W9-CZJ-538

# The Birth Day Letter

*June, 2005*
*To Susie —*
*my first book*
*but not my last, —*
*I hope!*

## By

## Marci Holland

*Marci Holland*

## Illustrated by

## Andrea Rinkel

authorHOUSE™

1663 LIBERTY DRIVE, SUITE 200
BLOOMINGTON, INDIANA 47403
(800) 839-8640
WWW.AUTHORHOUSE.COM

First published by AuthorHouse 02/23/05

ISBN: 1-4208-2921-1 (sc)
ISBN: 1-4208-2920-3 (dj)

Library of Congress Control Number: 2005900931

Printed in the United States of America
Bloomington, Indiana

This book is printed on acid-free paper.

# DEDICATED TO

MY PARENTS

HOWARD AND BETTY BRICKEY

# ACKNOWLEDGEMENTS

To: Ariel, Cynthia, Elva, and Eileen for their "thirteen year old" views. To the Alzheimer's Association, Heart of America Chapter, for their input and reading for content about Alzheimer's. To Friends: My long time Baker University girlfriends. "The Brady Bunch" couples' group. My book club members, Jeri, Sue, Ellen and Sandra who were the first to hear my desire to write this book. And to Arlene for her editing. To my family: My sister Linda, who shares my interest in this story. Shari, Michele and Mark who encouraged me and put up with listening to their mother's story for many hours on the phone. And especially my husband Ron, who did lots of editing and encouraged and supported me throughout the whole process. I thank them all! Marci Holland

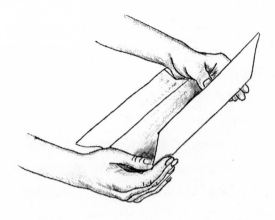

# JUNE 8

Dear CC,

Just when I think I'm going to quit this journal writing, something happens that I want to tell you about. So I've decided to write at least one more day!

**I finally made it to my 13th birthday!**

It is 3 a.m. and my four best friends, LeeAnn, Clarissa, Missy and Marie, are asleep on the floor in my bedroom. We had lots of fun tonight. Went out to dinner by ourselves at our favorite place called "50's Place" and had no parents telling us we were acting too silly or couldn't sing along with the music. We did the whole makeup thing like we do when we get to school, so we don't have to deal with mothers who freak out. We never have pizza, our favorite food, at this restaurant because they didn't make as much pizza in the 50's as they do now. Our favorite food here is a double stacked hamburger with everything. It's hard to eat but so good. We have fries and milk shakes or flavored colas. I wonder why they don't make hamburgers like that at all restaurants? Why just the 50's places? We love the poodle skirts the waitresses wear. And the music is so cool. Afterwards we came back to my house for more food, music and lots of girl talk, mostly about boys. We even called two. We each brought a DVD and watched 3 of them. Mine was the best but it missed the cut.

At breakfast Mom and Dad gave me a birthstone ring and it is so beautiful. Really looks grownup. I'm glad I was born in June because I love that pearl is the birthstone. My ring has a large pearl on a plain white gold band. They also gave me a gift card to buy DVD's. I'm excited to pick those out. Maybe LeeAnn can go with me. I got funny cards from my brothers from the thirteen-year old section of the card store. And money. I like that because I'm saving for my car in 3 years but nobody knows that.

Mom took me to lunch at her favorite restaurant in downtown Chicago. Mom made reservations so we could sit at the perfect table by the window. She said afterwards we could go shopping for birthday clothes at the store of my choice. I'm glad she said "my choice" because I can eat Mom's favorite food but I can't wear her choice of clothes. I wanted to go someplace hip!

Mom said she had a gift for me from my Grandmother Liz. I thought that was strange because Grandmother Liz has Alzheimer's and she doesn't even know who I am. Mother handed me a letter. In perfect script the envelope read:

*To Carly Elizabeth on her 13ᵗʰ Birthday*
*Written on the day of her birth*

I want to copy the letter because it is very special.

Dear Carly Elizabeth,

Your Grandpa and I are so happy to welcome you to our family. You are very special because you are our first granddaughter and named after me. Also we share the same birth month. I could never ask for a better gift. I have so much I want to tell you about your wonderful parents and your two brothers but you will find all that out soon enough.

So I will tell you a little about me. Even though we are two generations apart I think you will find over the years that there is a special bond between grandparents and grandchildren. We have enjoyed watching your brothers grow and get involved in sports, music and their assortment of collections. You will bring a whole new perspective with your interests that we will also enjoy. What is better than having two big brothers eleven and thirteen years older than you?

Celebrate all your relationships. You can learn so much from the good ones and even learn from the unhappy ones. Your family will be most important and supportive for you your entire life and especially your first several years. Then you will learn who you can depend on and be friends with in the world around you. Friends are really special because they will understand you, tell you what they think and be very loyal. They will be going through the same things as you and you will learn from each others' experiences.

I want to tell you about my best friend Molly Dash, she is like a sister to me. We have shared so many experiences with each other over these many years. We were neighbors growing up. We've talked about the Christmas we got our first bicycles and immediately broke the rules by riding them across the street instead of walking them across. We always remembered our favorite teachers, old friends and even our first kiss. Can you imagine your grandmother doing that? My favorite teacher was Miss Mulligan. She taught me self-respect, confidence and also 7th grade.

3

I always think of her when I get a little down and remember what she said about pulling yourself up by your bootstraps. I have always liked that figure of speech. Molly and I got into trouble a time or two much to our parents' disappointment. We took her parents' car out one night to cruise Main Street. We would never have been caught if she hadn't run over a curb and had a flat tire. We also shared the sad times. We were there for each other when our pets died. We cried when she got invited to a tea dance at school and I didn't. We supported each other when a classmate was killed in an accident. We cared about each other no matter what and we still do. And we love to look at the pictures of our weddings. We were each other's maid of honor and had the same shrimp colored dresses for our bride's maids. Molly got married 2 years after me and I almost wasn't able to be in her wedding because I was 8 months pregnant with your mother. And at that time it wasn't acceptable to be in that condition and be in a wedding. So our dresses were made like tents and I looked like a big balloon! Remind me to show you the pictures.

Having Molly as my college freshman roommate and being sorority sisters was such a wonderful fulfillment of our friendship. I hope you will be so lucky. We still keep in touch even though we both live in retirement homes, in different cities, and don't travel as much as we used to. They retired in the South and we wanted to stay close to family. And I'm so glad we did or I might not have seen you 2 hours old like I did this morning. How precious you are and we love you very much. Even your brothers were taken by your bright blue eyes and little heart shaped lips. You clasped on to their fingers when they held you. They assured you they would always be good big brothers for you. I hope they are.

You will be tempted many times in your growing up by situations and people that may try to influence you to make bad choices. Follow the good examples you have around you and stick to what you know is right.

I have thought about this letter for several months especially since I knew you would be a girl named Carly Elizabeth. I can't get used to this new technology that can tell what the baby will be before it is born. Very amazing. I have rewritten this several times because I wanted to say just the right things. I didn't want you to think I expected you to be or do anything other than what you choose to become.

I plan to give you this letter in person. We can go to lunch with your mom at your favorite place. (Grandpa says I'm the original lady of the "lets do lunch" bunch.) Thirteen years from now our lives will have changed and you will be a young woman. But my love for you will be as strong as it is today. I can't wait. It will be fun to share this letter with you and you can ask me questions about it and any other questions you might have. And I will want to hear everything about what it is like to be 13 in today's world.

I want you to meet Molly and have afternoon tea with us. Maybe you would like to bring a friend with you.

Much love, Grandmother Liz

| | |
|---|---|
| **Happy:** | Letter from Grandmother Liz |
| **Sad:** | Letter from Grandmother Liz |

# JUNE 9

Dear CC,

Okay, so I'm not going to stop writing my journal. I need it now more than ever. Ms. Lily was right. Once I started writing in a journal it became part of me. I never thought that I would still be doing something that I started in 5th grade. This is the ultimate homework assignment. Getting my laptop in my 6th grade year was the best thing ever. I can't imagine handwriting this now, especially after last night. I always seem to have so much to say. I wonder if there has ever been research about the fact that people think and write more since computers have become a fact of life. I keep meaning to go back and type in all my 5th grade journal writings that are still in a spiral notebook. I'll have to find it first.

Yesterday was a very emotional day for me. Happy, fun and sad all at the same time. Is it possible to have all those feelings in one day?

Today I asked Mother about Grandmother Liz' letter. She said she found it in Grandmother's things when they moved her out of the retirement home and into the nursing home.

After I read the letter yesterday I just sat very quietly and tears began to roll down my cheeks. Mom took my hand and her eyes told me how much she loved me. We didn't say anything for a long time. Then I asked her if she had read the letter and she said no. She said she didn't know what it said but did know that since it was written 13 years ago that whatever it said would be painful to read today. Mother also told me the birthstone ring they gave me belonged to Grandmother Liz. Since Grandmother and I share the same birth month she and Dad thought Grandmother Liz would like for me to have it. It was found in the same drawer as the letter that Grandmother had written me. That makes this ring even more meaningful. We didn't go shopping after lunch because I didn't feel very hip. I went home and got ready for the sleepover with my friends. I'm still tired from last night. I should have gone to bed when my girl friends did. Instead I took my laptop to the family room and wrote you. Then at 5:30 a.m. I tiptoed over 4 bodies and slept in my bed instead of on the floor with them. Before I fell asleep I wondered if one of these friends would become my Molly.

Happy:    Friends
Sad:      Alzheimer's

# JULY 19

Dear CC,

Grandpa died when I was 6 so I didn't know him very well. It seems like I remember him when I see the picture of me on his knee and riding the make believe horse. I remember going to their house for sleep overs and sleeping in the guest room on the 3rd floor. I was really scared up there by myself but acted as brave as I could. One night there was a thunderstorm and I was down in their room and in their bed before they knew what happened. Grandpa said he thought the ceiling had fallen in. I only had one set of grandparents. My father's parents died before I was born. But mother told me I was really spoiled by Grandmother Liz and Grandpa Jim. I got to have candy before dinner, eat ice cream cones at the mall and stay up late when I stayed with them. Mother said that was all right for grandparents to do but the rules were different at home. Soon after Grandpa died Grandmother Liz was diagnosed with Alzheimer's disease. She didn't have the constant care and help that Grandpa provided and went down hill very quickly. Mother kept telling me that Grandmother was forgetting a lot and I knew Mother was concerned. Even Grandpa thought Grandmother had some kind of dementia. I remember not being so concerned because I forgot things too. Like putting my toys away or helping set the table like most seven year olds. Mother said it's not like that. It starts out with not remembering the names of things or people. Later they wouldn't know what a toy or table are. I can't imagine such an illness.

Today Mother gave me a small photo album she has been working on of Grandmother Liz and me from the time I was born until I was six. And the picture of me on Grandpa's knee was in the album. Mother wanted me to see Grandmother with family, especially me, before she was diagnosed with Alzheimer's. I saw her having fun, being happy and enjoying her family.

She must have loved cooking because a lot of pictures are taken in her kitchen. In some I'm sitting on a tall stool right next to her so I can help. She made us matching aprons, one said, "Grandmother," and the other, "Grandmother's Little Helper". I wonder if Mother found those when they were moving Grandmother Liz? Grandmother seemed to like to hold my hand in the pictures. I liked that. I wish I had gotten to know Grandmother Liz better before she got sick. Or I'd rather she hadn't got sick at all.

Mother decided not to give me the pictures after I read the letter because she thought that might be too much all at once. I appreciated that. I thanked her and told her the pictures mean a lot to me. I couldn't stop looking at them because Grandmother Liz looked so different than she does now. Can a disease change someone that much? I have a lot to learn about Alzheimer's disease.

Happy:     Pictures
Sad:       Pictures

# AUGUST 2

Dear CC,

Today not much happened. Thank goodness. I have just been thinking a lot. I have thought about my favorite teacher Ms. Lily, who taught 5th grade. She is the only teacher I've had so far that has asked her classes to call her by her first name. She never said why but it wasn't hard to figure out. Her last name was Pond. Her Mom must have been delirious or had a weird sense of humor. It would have been awful if she had taught biology!

My friends and I had another name for Ms. Lily that we liked better. When Ms. Lily would get frustrated with us or with something she was doing she would say "horsefeathers". She would say it in almost a whisper like it was a bad word. After class one day we asked her why she said "horsefeathers"—and so quietly. She told us that when she told her grandmother she was going to be a teacher the only thing her grandmother said was, "Oh Dear."

Thinking that was not a very positive response, she asked her about it. Her grandmother said, "You may have trouble in a classroom with your potty mouth. Why don't you say 'horsefeathers' instead of the bad word you are thinking? It kept me out of a lot of trouble and it probably will you too."

Realizing that was a good idea, Ms. Lily substituted "horsefeathers" at the appropriate times and said it softly like it was a bad word. Ms. Lily said she blames the boy that lived down the street from her while growing up for her potty mouth. I think everyone should have a boy down the street to blame for shortcomings! Good excuse Ms. Horsefeathers!

The idea of writing something about myself three times a week seemed overwhelming at the time. But Ms. Lily said it was a requirement of her English Class. I wanted an "A" in the class so I followed her directions. Ms. Lily said a journal or diary is personal writings of daily events, usually brief. It's the brief part I've never understood. My days need more than a paragraph of explanation. She said people doing genealogy research read old diaries and letters to find out about family histories. Ms. Lily said friends of hers who take trips keep a journal of the places they visit—and then show her the pictures they took. I think Ms. Lily is more into the writing part.

Ms. Horsefeathers was always showing us examples of our lessons or bringing to class someone that could tell us experiences they have had to make our writing lesson come to life. My friend LeeAnn was afraid to write about reptiles or brown bears because Ms. Horsefeathers would find a person who would bring reptiles or brown bears to class. We learned to never underestimate Ms. Lily.

She brought a letter to class one day that was from Christa McAuliffe, the first teacher to fly in space. I have since read books about her. Ms. Lily was in middle school when the Challenger blew up on take off. Her 6th grade teacher had written Ms. McAuliffe a letter and told her that they were keeping personal journals in her class. They read that she was going to keep a journal on her space flight and would share it afterwards. The class received that letter the day before the accident. In the letter she thanked them for their letter and said it was exciting to be representing the teaching profession. Christa McAuliffe hand wrote a P.S. that said, "Have your students keep their diaries-we don't want to lose all that social history."

Some students thought Ms. Horsefeathers was just showing off or made up stuff to impress us. But I didn't feel that way. I always thought she was sincere and just enjoyed being a teacher. I learned a lot from her and tried not to be her favorite student but I think I was! That is a fast track to disaster.

She wanted us to name our journals. We could call it anything we wanted, as long as there was no foul language. I wanted to keep mine simple. Since my name starts with a C and my brothers are Charlie and Chris, I thought I should have a C name for my journal. I couldn't think of any C name that sounded right so I named it CC. That means Carly's Copy. It makes sense to me. Reporters write "copy" for the newspaper. Maybe I'll be a reporter some day.

Ms. Lily also wanted us to write, at the end of each entry, a happy and sad word that applied to what we had just written. I always find it easier to write the happy word.

I asked Mother if she ever kept a journal. She said no, she never had a teacher that assigned personal writings like that. She did say she keeps a small calendar in her purse and writes down the things she needs to do or places she needs to go. And it was a handy place to keep family birthdays. Then she keeps the calendars at the end of the year and can go back at least 20 years to see what she did on a certain day. I want to find the calendar that has the day I was born. Wonder if she felt like writing on that day? Her only problem is sometimes she forgets to look at her calendar and doesn't make it to the appointment she had written down. It has been suggested to Mom that she use a PDA to keep track of her activities. She said she's hasn't gone high tech yet. I'm thinking probably never! I'm going to stick to my journal writing for now, at least until high school.

School starts in about 3 weeks and I'm ready for my last year in Central Middle School. Mother asked what I was going to wear the first day of school.

I said, "What?" She asked if I wanted something special. I said special is a pair of jeans and a tee shirt. I asked Mother where she got that funny idea. She told me Grandmother Liz always made the first day of school special. They went shopping for a new outfit. I said that was nice for you but my friends would laugh me out of 8th grade if I did that. Especially if I wore something besides jeans.

Mom said, "Just thought I'd ask."

"Thanks, but no thanks." Sometimes Mother and I aren't on the same wavelength.

Happy:     Teachers
Sad:       That I don't have Ms. Lily for a teacher this year

# AUGUST 27

Dear CC,

School has started. I'm in all the classes I wanted. LeeAnn and I have lockers in the same hall. That's better than last year when we were on different floors.

It's Saturday and this morning Mom asked me if I'd like to go see Grandmother Liz with her. She goes every week and I have been going only occasionally since I was seven. Grandmother doesn't know me and I don't know what to say to her so I end up talking to the nurses or family members who visit other patients. But I have been thinking about visiting Grandmother Liz and decided to go. Mother may have thought since Grandmother Liz was such a large part of my birthday that I would want to visit her more.

When we got to the nursing home I asked Mom if she would just drop me off and I'd call her when I was ready to leave. She seemed very surprised but agreed. She wanted to know if I would be all right. I said I think so.

I found Grandmother in the lounge area of her unit sitting with her head down like she was asleep. I tapped her on the shoulder and startled her and she looked very scared.

I said, "Hi, Grandmother Liz, how are you?" She continued to stare at me and said nothing.

I said, "I'm Carly, your granddaughter. Your daughter, Phyllis, couldn't come today. Is it okay for me to visit you?" She held out her hand and wanted to stand up. We walked to her room and she sat in her chair. It was the only piece of furniture from her former home that was moved to the nursing home. And it had always been a favorite chair of hers. Mother said Grandmother called it her "Everything Chair." I would like for Grandmother Liz to be able to tell me what that meant.

I sat on a folding chair that was in the room. She held my hands and I said, "I want to thank you for the letter you wrote me on the day I was born. Mother gave it to me on my 13th birthday." I asked her if she could say my name. She didn't respond. I said Carly several times and then she said, "Carly" very softly back to me.

I said, "Do you know who I am?" She shook her head no. I asked her if it was okay for me to visit her. She just nodded. I decided to tell her about my family and school and was hoping I would say a word that she would recognize. I was getting very few responses from her. She moved her fingers over my hands and looked down at them and then at me. I gave her a hug but she did not give me one back. I said I would be back to see her. Her only response was a pat on my hand.

My tears came after I left her room. I had so much to share with Grandmother Liz and she didn't understand or even have the ability to verbally express herself. And I was selfish enough to want her to know and love me like she wrote about in her letter. It was then that I realized I needed to lower my expectations and go for some very small response. This is not what Ms. Lily taught me. But on the other hand I think she would be pleased that I saw the need to do this so I could have some satisfaction with this new relationship with my grandmother.

Our ride home was quiet and Mother said she understood and knew it was a difficult visit. She asked if I wanted to visit Grandmother Liz again by myself. I immediately said, "Next Saturday."

I had a fun weekend with my friends. And according to my friend LeeAnn, or Annie as I sometimes call her, there is a certain boy who says he likes me. This could be interesting.

I could not quit thinking about Grandmother Liz. I just thought about her patting my hands and looking at them. And I want to know about the "Everything Chair."

Happy:      School
Sad:        Grandmother Liz

# SEPTEMBER 9

Dear CC,

There is excitement in the air! My oldest brother, who is 26, has announced his engagement and the wedding date has been set. Mother is beside herself. She's already worrying about what to wear. I said, "Mom, cool it!" LeeAnn told me when her brother got married her mom wore beige and kept quiet. Mom is also worrying about having the bride's parents for dinner, if her family will have a shower for the bride and if I'll be in the wedding.

I said, "It sounds like the only thing you need to worry about is planning a couple of dinners, one to meet the parents and one for the rehearsal dinner. And the bride will probably tell you what to wear. Just hang in." The wedding is in June so Mom has lots of time to anticipate and worry about everything.

I'm happy for my brother. He's a great guy but the spoiled child in the family according to me! I didn't think people 26 could be spoiled. He does drive my friends and me places and take us to our favorite place to eat, which right now is "Wanna Burger". He always says, "Wanna what?" I can't see him doing that with a wife.

My other brother lives in Galveston and doesn't come home as often. He got married, four years ago, at age 20. They had a small wedding on a beach somewhere so I didn't get to be a junior bride's maid and Mother was disappointed. I'm waiting to be an aunt but he tells me I can stop thinking about that for a while.

I have always considered myself an only child. My brothers might be surprised to hear that. They were 11 and 13 when I was born and being the only girl I was spoiled, or so I'm told. By the time my brothers started paying attention to me they were ready to go to college or work. Maybe all children in a family are spoiled in their special way by their parents and they just never compare notes. Probably better that way.

I have decided being 13 isn't so bad. I like 8th grade and that is top dog at my middle school. We boss the poor 6th graders around. They are such babies. I have signed up to play volleyball and I joined Spanish club and book club. I'm not crazy about the book club sponsor but I love to read so I plan to stick with it.

I have been thinking about what area I could be involved in that would help my grandmother. Maybe I could do some volunteering in an area that would mean something to older people like my grandmother. I talked to my school counselor and she suggested I try and get some friends interested and we could start a club for students who want to do volunteer work. I know they do that in high school and I want to be involved in it next year. I decided to do it so now I have a new project to work on. I love projects. I called LeeAnn immediately. My excitement was stopped temporarily because she was talking to Robbie and said she'd call me back. I hate call waiting.

Mother showed me the newsletter that was in the mail today. It was from the nursing home where Grandmother lives. There was an announcement about a new support group for families of patients who have some form of dementia. Mom wanted to know if

I would be interested in going with her to the three sessions. I said yes. Maybe the more I know the more I can understand and not be so frustrated with the disease Grandmother Liz has. Next week is the first session.

In the meantime Mother is having a garage sale this weekend and LeeAnn and I said we'd help her. I suggested she just take the stuff to a second hand store. She said it was more fun to have a sale. How can anyone think standing in the garage all day trying to sell junk is fun? Only mothers I guess. I'd rather be grounded for the weekend.

Happy:     Weddings
Sad:       Garage sales

# DECEMBER 8

Dear CC,

I haven't written in my journal for 3 months. I have been so busy with school. All my teachers think they are the only one giving home work assignments. I really like the activities I'm involved in. I like 8th grade a lot but I probably don't have to do everything in one semester.

Mother tripped on a small throw rug in the kitchen and fell and broke her wrist. She said she tried to catch herself and her wrist just gave out. She had a cast put on it and was slowed down only slightly. She is left-handed which is good because she broke her right wrist. I asked her if she was going to move the throw rug. She said, "No. I'll just be more careful."

I have been helping Mom a lot. Dad is helping a lot, too, so between the two of us we can get Mother's work done around the house. I've decided I hate housework worse than homework. With homework I usually learn something I didn't know before. Can't say that after running the vacuum. Mom can't tie her tennis shoes or button her coat. I tease her about that.

Today is my 13½ birthday. My Dad said they always celebrated that date in his family when he was growing up. A little odd, I think, but we celebrate it in our family anyway. The day of the half birthday, the half birthday person owns the day. After school my choice was to invite LeeAnn to go out to dinner with us. We went to a vegetarian restaurant and had delicious roasted veggies, pasta in a cream sauce, stuffed mushrooms and hot fudge sundaes. I know Dad thought the best part was dessert. He was a good sport but was probably wishing for a meat and potato meal. If he didn't like my choice he shouldn't have shared his half birthday idea with me! I even got gifts. LeeAnn gave me a little red book for telephone numbers. She wrote some numbers down for me, the boys she thought I liked! Mom and Dad gave me a TV with a DVD player for my room. I was very pleased but didn't tell them all my friends have had one for years! I wonder if LeeAnn suggested it, just kidding! Now I can watch my DVD's in my room instead of the family room.

LeeAnn and I have found 11 people who are interested in organizing a volunteer club at school. We have to write a mission statement and go through all the hoops with the administration to get it started. We asked our 8th grade history teacher to be our sponsor. I wish Ms. Lily taught in Middle School. She would be a great sponsor for our club. At our first meeting we will elect officers. I'm very excited about this.

I have been to visit Grandmother Liz three times by myself. We sat on the patio outside her unit one day. We watched butterflies in the flowers. She never said anything but she would point at them when they flew near her. Each visit I tell her about her letter and about my school and all about being 13. And each time she just wants to hold my hands. She always looks at my birthstone ring and puts her fingers on it. The last time I was there I thought I saw a faint smile when she reached for it and then looked at me. But then that may be just wishful thinking on my part. I want so much for Grandmother Liz to know who I am.

Mother asked me tonight if she could read the letter Grandmother Liz gave me 6 months ago. I said of course. I know it will be as hard for her to read as it was for me. Seeing her own mother disappear right before her eyes has to be heartbreaking. I hope Mother can see the good memories and be happy that Grandmother Liz knew me before she got sick. I don't want Mother to be sad but I know she will be. Maybe we can talk about the letter sometime.

I asked Mother why she waited so long to ask to read the letter. She said because she felt that it was just between Grandmother Liz and me. She also said she had to admit that she knew it would be hard for her to read it. When she thought about the day I was born everyone was so happy. It breaks her heart to think that her mother was writing a letter to her granddaughter on that day. And then not be able to share it 13 years later. Mom went on to say that she saw, over the last several months, how I was accepting the letter and just hoped she could do as well.

She said, "It's just time."

I was just happy she asked.

I love my computer. I can be in bed with it, write you, watch my TV and wait for my cordless to ring. All this after homework of course! Good night CC.

Happy:     Families
Sad:        Mom reading my letter

# JANUARY 13

Dear CC,

The holidays are over and I'm back in my routine. My brothers were here and that was fun. Mother's wrist has pretty much healed and I'm not in the kitchen as much now. I think Mom and Dad got tired of frozen pizza. They never complained. Dad got real good with pancakes so we had variety! The throw rug is still in the kitchen.

Ruben talked to me today at school. That's cool. He told LeeAnn he liked me so I was prepared. There is an 8th grade Valentine dance next month so maybe he's talking to me before he asks me. Hope so. I thought about calling him tonight but I lost my nerve. Also Mother would weird out on me if she knew I wanted to do that. How come everyone else's mom doesn't care? I hope he asks me soon so I'll have plenty of time to pick out the perfect dress.

Mom and I went to our first support group meeting tonight at the nursing home. I learned a lot I didn't know about dementia and specifically about Alzheimer's. The same disease affects everyone differently. All patients have different degrees of memory loss. They cannot remember and can't remember that they can't remember. They may ask the same question over and over believing it's the first time they've asked it.

Their speech becomes incoherent or their words don't always fit the situation. On a visit with Grandmother Liz she tried to talk but said a few words that were disconnected and didn't make any sense. I would try to figure out what she wanted to say and answer her and if it wasn't what she wanted to hear it only frustrated her.

Mother was concerned because Grandmother Liz used to be very conscious of how she dressed. Now her clothes are mismatched, unclean, too big or layered four deep. Mother asked the nurse about that and she explained that they want the residents to do what they can for themselves and if she wants to dress herself they let her. The nurse said they would try to locate dirty clothes to be washed. Sometimes patients hide things to protect them and that makes it hard for the staff to find.

Other family members had questions and I learned a lot from them. I found I was comparing Grandmother Liz to other patients. Some are not as bad and lots are worse than she is. I guess that's what the future is for my grandmother.

Mother and I were glad we went. On the way home I asked Mother what she thought about Grandmother Liz' letter. She looked at me and said she feels sorry for me. I told her I feel sorry for Grandmother. Then she explained that she wishes that I could have known my grandmother as she was when I was born. I agreed but that isn't possible so I have to do the best I can with the way she is now. I think mother and I accept grandmother's illness on different levels. Mother's concern now is for me. That makes me mad that

Mother feels sorry for me and not for Grandmother Liz. I'm going to be okay, especially as I learn more about the disease. I just have to come to an understanding that this is the disease Grandmother will have for the rest of her life. And I wonder how long she will live? I want to ask mother that but decided now wasn't the time. She suggested I talk to my brothers about Grandmother Liz because they got to be with her during her healthy years. That was a good idea. I reminded Mother that that is why she gave me the pictures. So I could see her before the illness. She agreed. Mother did say that the letter was very sweet and something to treasure. She said she didn't know her mother had written it on the day I was born and had never mentioned it. She was glad that they found it in Grandmother's things. She also said that Grandmother Liz would be very proud of me today. Yikes! I'm always nervous when Mother says something like that. I thanked Mother again for the little picture album. She just smiled.

Happy:     Talking to Mother
Sad:       Mad at Mother for feeling sorry for me

# JANUARY 18

Dear CC,

Today Volunteer Club met after school. There were 8 girls and 5 boys. We elected officers and I am the president. Brady is vice president and Missy is recording secretary. That will be the hardest job. She'll have to record the hours of volunteering that are turned in. We set up a box with cards so that each person can write down their hours after they do them. Mr. Parks, our sponsor, said we could leave the box in his classroom.

We thought of a slogan for our club. G.O.T. means Giving Our Time. We made large buttons to wear and hope that other classmates will ask us about it and want to join us. The buttons have a clock face for the background with G.O.T. printed on top. Missy's art class helped us with materials and printing. It seems that everyone is wearing some kind of button promoting the latest event. Right now the whole school is voting for the two students with the best personality that will be announced at the dance coming up. I'm still hoping Ruben has my phone number.

All of the club members said what they would like to do for their volunteer hours. Some wanted to baby-sit after school. Some wanted to do yard work for elderly neighbors. And others wanted to go to the nursing home with me and visit with the patients. I told them the nurses had certain people they would suggest to visit. Some like to be read to, have someone to walk with or just sit with them. I think that is the hardest part. I think I have to be doing something or my visit doesn't count. We planned to meet in 2 weeks. I feel really good that we have started this club. I think it is very worthwhile.

I went over to LeeAnn's house tonight to work on an assignment about consumer problems for Home Ec. That didn't take as long as it did to decide how to make Ruben ask me to the Valentine dance. Robbie has asked LeeAnn and she has been looking for her dress but hasn't found one yet. Robbie said his older brother would take them. And if Ruben asks me we can go with them. I like that better than parents driving. It's always embarrassing for a parent to drive us but if they have to we have them drop us off at the end of the block so it isn't so obvious. Then they wait, of course, until we get inside. I understand now why being 16 is so important! I've heard some students are renting limos for the dance. I really want to save that experience for high school—and my wedding, if limos are still popular by then! Besides my parents wouldn't let me do that anyway.

When I got home Dad said that a boy named Ruben called. I tried not to act too excited. I asked Dad what he said to him. He said he told him to never call me again.

I yelled, "DAD". He started laughing. I wish I didn't always fall for Dad's teasing. He then said Ruben would see me at school tomorrow and would talk to me then. Now I'm wondering what kind of dress I want for the dance. There couldn't possibly be any other reason he would want to talk to me.

Happy:     G.O.T.

Sad:        Dad's teasing

# JANUARY 19

Dear CC,

I couldn't believe it. I woke up this morning with a slight fever and cough. Mother said she was calling school to excuse my absence. I went into a 10 minute explanation of why I couldn't miss school and I wasn't legally sick. I just had a little cough.

But she called anyway. I hate missing school. Mother must think it would make her look bad if I went to school with a cough. Mothers, Mothers, Mothers! They worry too much.

I stayed home until after lunch. I was a good patient for half a day. I took cough medicine, took a nap and hid the thermometer. I told Mom I had to go back in the afternoon so I could get all my assignments that I missed. I had another reason, too.

I saw LeeAnn and she had already heard that I missed Ruben's call. That's why I can't miss school! After school I was at my locker getting my books for homework when Ruben walked up and asked if I was okay.

I said, "Yes, why?"

"Well, you weren't at school this morning and I thought maybe your Dad grounded you because I called last night." We both laughed. He invited me to the dance and wanted to know what color dress I would be wearing. I said I have no idea but would let him know when I found one. I could hardly wait to tell LeeAnn.

Mother and I got an invitation to a shower for Chris' fiancé, Abby. I have been around her quite a bit and like her a lot. She and my brother seemed made for each other. They both have outgoing personalities and have tons of friends. She is a social worker and Chris is an attorney. They are people people. Mom wants me to go shopping with her for our shower gifts. I said she could get them and I'd sign the card. I got one of those "roll her eyes looks"!

I talked to LeeAnn tonight and we're going shopping for our dance dresses on Saturday afternoon. We want to find the ones we like by ourselves and then take our moms for the buying part. That way we can try on all kinds of dresses knowing we would never buy them but could see how they look. With Mom I would have to try on only the dresses that were possibilities to buy. I wonder if Mother ever played dress up?

On Saturday morning Mom and I went to see Grandmother Liz. She was in her room in her chair holding a stuffed animal. I told her about my school and being invited to a dance. She reached for my hand and touched my pearl ring. Mother asked her if she remembered that ring. Grandmother just looked at Mother very confused. Later we walked with her down the hall and had a snack together and then left. Mom said she was so glad I was willing to visit Grandmother Liz. I told her I would do the same thing if she didn't have Alzheimer's, it would just be at her retirement home. I agreed we would have had real conversations instead of one sided like now, but I need to tell her about my life. She doesn't understand but it makes me feel better that I'm sharing with her. She deserves to know.

On our way home we talked about the "Everything Chair". Mother said she remembers it being stacked with clean clothes to be folded or groceries to be put away. One time it was a bed for a sick kitty that Grandmother was helping get well. It was the chair in the picture of Grandmother holding me when I was a baby with Grandpa standing by her. It was the chair that my two brothers were found jumping up and down on. And it was the chair that I spilled a glass of red punch on. Mother said that was the most difficult clean up job she ever had. Mother said Grandmother used to say some people called special chairs "Company Chairs" but she liked "Everything Chair" better.

Mother dropped me off at the mall to meet LeeAnn. We decided we would be "Mall Dolls"! We've heard that expression but have no idea what it means or how to act like one! We figured it meant girls who hang out at the mall all the time, which we don't, but we could try it for one afternoon. We had lunch in the food court. Then went to several stores to find the perfect dress. Of course LeeAnn decided on the first one she tried on. That left me the rest of the afternoon to find one. She got to try on dresses for fun. We had a good time together. She asked me questions about my Grandmother Liz and said she wanted to go to the nursing home to do some volunteer hours. She said she didn't know anything about Alzheimer's but wanted to learn. I suggested she start visiting with patients that could talk to her then see if she wanted to visit an Alzheimer's patient. It is really difficult when the patient doesn't talk to you. And most Alzheimer's patients that can carry on a conversation aren't in a nursing home yet; unless they hit people or have some unrelated medical problem. LeeAnn decided she would go with me next time I went.

I finally found my dress. I think LeeAnn was about to give up on me. It is hot pink. It has a long straight taffeta skirt and the top has spaghetti straps. A light pink sash ties in a bow at the back. I found pink shoes that match perfectly. Before we called our moms to come see our dresses I picked out several CD's and DVD's with my birthday gift card. I thought I had lost it but found it recently in the bottom of my book bag. I clean it out usually once during the school year and I'm glad I did. Mother had asked me more than once what I bought with the card. I told her I was waiting for new releases. I like what I call mood music. LeeAnn calls it mushy music. That is the only area I can think of that we don't agree on. I listen to her country western but prefer my slow and mellow songs. My movie selections are different than hers too. She's into what I call a scary stage and I'm into Broadway musicals. That's what I like about LeeAnn. We can disagree and not get mad at each other. I guess you'd say we respect each other's opinions.

Our mothers came to the mall and bought the dresses we picked out. And I have to say there was no debate or disagreement over our choices. We were relieved because we just weren't up to discussing money, fabric, style or explain why we liked the dresses we picked. I got the new pair of shoes, too. I'm all set for the dance.

All I have to do now is tell Ruben it is hot pink!

LeeAnn and I think we saw some "Mall Dolls" and decided we didn't need to be like that. They were high school age girls carrying lots of shopping bags and looking like they weren't having any fun. We have fun just window-shopping. We can try on shoes or hats and think we've really had a good time, especially when we try on hats and laugh ourselves silly.

Happy:     Friends

Sad:       Grandmother Liz

# JANUARY 24

Dear CC,

I went with Mother tonight to the last family support group at the nursing home. I missed the second one because I was legally sick. I had a cough!

I learned some more interesting facts about dementia. Like a visitor should never argue with an Alzheimer's patient. Mother said she did that when Grandmother first started showing signs of dementia. But the patient can't reason or even remember what they are saying so to argue is pointless. And it only gets everyone upset. Never tell a patient they forgot. Their whole illness is based on forgetting, we shouldn't question their memory—or lack of. I agreed with the social worker that Alzheimer's disease is a very difficult disease to deal with. When the well person knows what day it is and the patient tells you you are wrong there is no way you can convince them or make them believe. I think frustration has to be the biggest enemy of anyone dealing with an Alzheimer's patient. I know it has been for me.

The social worker did say we can do things to help ourselves. We can repeat what we say in short sentences. Agree with the patient or distract them to a different activity. The hardest thing I heard tonight was to be cheerful and reassuring and just go with the flow. I finally realized I have to do what I can to help me, knowing that it won't make any difference to Grandmother. Just being myself is all I can give to Grandmother Liz. She expects nothing.

On the way home Mother said she is very proud of me and thinks I have an understanding of Grandmother Liz way beyond my years. She said she couldn't ask for a better daughter. I told her I was just being a granddaughter. It just happens that I have a grandmother that can't be a grandmother.

I told Mother I feel a lot of anger with the disease Alzheimer's. Why does my grandmother have it? How did she get it? Can I get it? Why isn't there a cure? Mother looked at me and said if she could answer those questions she would be famous. I told her I don't need for her to be famous. I just want answers. Knowing I was angry and serious with my questions she suggested I contact the State Department of Aging and our local Alzheimer's Association. Both of those agencies could give me information and maybe answers to my questions. I just didn't feel very hopeful tonight. I still think Grandmother Liz doesn't know who I am. Or does she?

Happy:     My Mother
Sad:       Her Mother

# JANUARY 25

Dear CC,

I'm exhausted tonight. After our meeting last night I stayed up very late studying for a test I had today. I hope I did okay. School seems to be overtaking me right now. Either I'm getting way behind or they are trying to see if we can develop study habits for high school. I know I am more involved than I have ever been in outside school activities. After school clubs, going to ball games, volunteering and just being with my friends. I want to manage it all and make good grades too. Eighth grade must be one big test. Hope I pass!

After school today was G.O.T. We all wore our buttons. Two more students wanted to join. We had a total of 29 hours reported. One of the boys did some yard clean up for an elderly neighbor even though he said it was boring. Troy played gin rummy with a man at the nursing home who had a broken hip. He said he'd never played it before but Mr. Williams wanted to teach him and then Mr. Williams beat him 3 games. Troy said he's going to be ready for him next time.

Jose pushed Mr. Larson in his wheelchair in the neighborhood around the nursing home. He wants to get credit with his track coach as well as G.O.T. He figures he walked several miles before Mr. Larson asked him if he was tired.

Jose said, "No. Do you want to go around again?"

He said, "Sure. And make it three square blocks instead of two."

Jose said, "Sure." Jose told us he thought to himself: "I have all the cracks in the sidewalk memorized in the two square blocks. Now I have new material." We all laughed and teased him about wanting to double his hours just because Mr. Lawson was a very large man. At least 300 pounds, he said. We told him whining didn't count.

LeeAnn was asked to read to Mrs. Bryant who has low vision. LeeAnn was thinking newspaper or magazine. But the lady wanted her to read her favorite cookbook. Mrs. Bryant said she can't cook and can't read but it would sure be nice if LeeAnn would read her some recipes. It would bring back so many memories. So Mrs. Bryant gave LeeAnn her cookbook and told her which recipes she wanted to hear. LeeAnn said it seemed really strange at first but the more she thought about it, what better way to recall family gatherings and celebrations than with food? In fact, LeeAnn said she liked the sound of the Most Delicious Cinnamon Roll Ever so she copied it down. We told her she needed to make them for the club so we could be the judge to see if that was the correct name for the recipe.

Others shared how they were getting their hours and seemed excited about their volunteering. Except for Bobby. He hadn't started yet---but was going to soon. So our club was complete. We have variety.

This is the last week to vote on a boy and a girl with the best personality. I'm voting for Ruben and LeeAnn. Not just because they are my friends but they are both friendly to everyone. They are well liked and they go out of their way to include students who may not be as popular. They don't show off or have an "attitude". They are just fun to be around. I'm glad they aren't going to the dance together. Robbie and I would be out of luck. I wonder if the candidates vote for themselves? I'll have to ask LeeAnn.

I don't include my visits with my grandmother as my volunteer hours but I do get mine at the nursing home. I went to the unit where the patients are there temporarily. They may have had surgery and have no one at home to take care of them or they had something happen that their care giver couldn't handle by themselves. That was the case for Mrs. Horton.

The nurse told me she was in great need of someone to talk to and do a few things for her. Well, this was the person for me. I needed action. I just didn't know I would get almost more than I could handle! Most of our first visit was her telling me how she got two broken arms. She said it was a freak accident. She was putting her miniature china dolls on their shelf after she had dusted the display case and she accidentally missed the last step on the step stool as she was stepping on the floor. She fell sideways and broke her left arm and grabbed the display case for support and pulled it over on her and broke her right arm. She then lay there and cried and cursed herself because she also broke a whole shelf of her dolls. She knew her arms could be fixed but not the dolls. She was sure her collection was ruined. Her husband thought he heard a sound and came in the room to find her on the floor. He did not say what she wanted to hear so she told him to shut up and call 911. When they got to the emergency room someone asked her if she was right handed or left handed.

She said she just yelled, "What difference does it make?"

38

I was thankful that Mother just broke one wrist. But Mother isn't Mrs. Horton.

Mrs. Horton gave me some money because she wants me to pick out some pretty note cards for her. She wants me to write the members of her garden club and thank them for the food for her husband and the flowers for her. I'm thinking one note would cover the whole club but she said she wanted to send notes to all 9 members. I didn't count on having homework with my volunteering. I'll find some cards with flowers on them.

It was time for me to leave and a nurse came in with some ice cream for an afternoon snack. Mrs. Horton asked if I would feed it to her. I said sure. I just hope Mom doesn't mind waiting for me.

I saw Ruben after school and said "hot pink" and he gave a thumbs up.

Happy:     Bringing Back Memories
Sad:        Having No Memory At All

# FEBRUARY 2

Dear CC,

I woke up this morning wondering again how I can help Grandmother Liz understand who I am. I think too much of her memory has been erased for her to remember my relationship to her. But I keep thinking there has to be a thread of something that will help her remember that she has a granddaughter. It's not like she has 10 granddaughters. I'm the only one. My enemy has attacked me this morning. Frustration!

Last night my friends and I went to a high school basketball game. We played like we were freshman but I'm sure we didn't fool anyone. Especially not the boys! Clarissa has an older sister so she and her boyfriend let us hang out with them. We tried not to be too silly and loud. But just looking around at the high school students we thought they were acting awfully silly. Stupid in fact. So we figured we looked pretty good. Maybe high school won't be as hard to adjust to as I thought.

We enjoyed watching the cheerleaders. Some of my friends want to try out this summer. I haven't decided if I will or not. I like to watch sports and try to know something about how the game is played. Basketball is probably the easiest to understand. I remember when

I was in 5th grade and our gym teacher introduced her classes to tennis. It took me months to figure out the scoring. I still think it is complicated. I can't imagine having a date with a high school guy next year and going to a sporting event and not know what is going on. I have a thing about looking stupid. Especially around boys.

Today was the shower for Abby. She came over to the house to go with us. While she was here she asked me if I would be a jr. bridesmaid in her and Chris' wedding. I said I would love to. My brother looked at me and seemed so proud. I don't feel any more comfortable with him looking that way than I do with Mother.

I asked Abby if her bridesmaid's dresses were going to be shrimp colored. Chris said, "Where did that come from?"

I said, "Grandmother Liz had shrimp colored dresses in her wedding and I thought maybe it was popular again."

Chris said, "Assuming it was popular then—100 years ago!" Abby explained that they are having a black and white wedding. And she and I will be the only ones in white. The other bridesmaids will wear long black dresses with white sashes. I could see the wheels going around in Mother's head and was wondering what she would say about that.

I looked at her as she said, "That sounds beautiful." Mother asked what she and Sue should wear. Abby said a long black dress of their choice. She said Mother could talk to her mom at the shower today. Just work it out not to choose the same dress.

Abby said, "Unless you both want to wear the same dress."

I thought, "Oh please!"

The shower was fun, the punch and fancy food were very good and Abby got tons of gifts. She is having 7 bridesmaids and they were all there. I wonder how many sleep overs they've had together? I do well to manage with only 4 good friends. But I haven't been to high school, college or out working yet. I guess you gather up a few more friends along the way. There was lots of laughing over gifts and joking going around that was way over my head, which was probably just as well. Thirteen year olds are pretty much babies around 25 year olds.

I had met Abby's parents and sister when they came to our house for dinner. But I convinced my mother that I didn't belong at that dinner party so she agreed I could stay and say hello and then go to Clarissa's house for the evening. Mother said it went well and she thinks she and Mrs. Barry, rather Sue, will get along just fine. Good thing. Because I think they are pretty much stuck with the in-law thing.

I have another shower to go to with mostly our relatives. Mother says I have to go to all the wedding events since I'm in the wedding party. Mother and I are hosting a bridal tea two days before the wedding at a local hotel. Maybe I will get to buy another new dress.

Chris stayed with us over the weekend. I asked him if he would go with me to see Grandmother Liz. He agreed and we had a good talk on the way over. He has good memories of visiting our grandparents while he was growing up. He and Grandfather would go fishing and camp out. Grandmother would fix big meals for them and complain when they would bring in fish or a bird for her to cook. Chris said he liked to look at their old pictures of past generations. So Grandfather gave the albums to Chris and decided he could become the family genealogist. I told him I wanted to see them. He said in about 40 years he should have them in some kind of order that would make sense. I guess Grandfather didn't take his job as a genealogist very seriously. But Chris said he loved fishing and that was his real hobby.

We went in to see Grandmother Liz. She was resting in her room in her "Everything Chair". She looked at Chris first and reached for him, he gave her a big hug. I gave her a hug but again no response. Chris talked about his and Abby's wedding. He asked Grandmother if her "Everything Chair" was comfortable.

He said, "Maybe it got new springs after Charlie and I jumped it to death." His saying things like that make me uncomfortable. It's like making fun of the person because they can't understand what you are saying. She certainly can't respond.

I said, "Cool it Chris." I talked about Grandmother's wedding, the shrimp colored dresses and about Molly. Grandmother looked at me and took my hand. My talking just didn't make any sense to her. So guess I shouldn't have been so worried about what Chris was saying to her.

We heard a lot of noise in the hall and there were a couple of small children running and being loud. Their mother had not caught up to them yet to give them the word about being quiet. The little girl, about 5, wandered into Grandmother's room.

Grandmother Liz looked at her and said, "Carly" as plain as day. I looked at Chris and he looked at me and we were speechless. I just realized she only knows me from the time before she got sick. This 13 year old person is a complete stranger to her because she never knew me at this age. I was beginning to make some small sense of this terrible illness. Nothing about it has ever made sense to me before but this one situation seemed so obvious. The little girl ran out of the room as fast as she came in. And nothing else was said. We walked in the hall with Grandmother Liz for several minutes and then told her goodbye.

On the way home I was still shocked with what Grandmother Liz had said. I told Chris that was the only time in the last six months that I had heard her say any word voluntarily. I asked Chris how he thought I could transfer that word to me. He said it would be difficult. Maybe I could show her pictures of me at 5 or 6 and say, "Carly" and then point to me. I have no idea how the mind works with Alzheimer's. But I'm not going to quit trying to help her know who I am. I think I have a plan that might work.

I was so glad Chris was with me today or I don't think anyone would believe me if I told them what Grandmother said when she saw the little girl.

I enjoyed my time today with my big brother. It isn't often that I get this much time with him by myself. When he was home it was usually connected with business and he'd have dinner with us and that would be about it.

I pointed out to him that he was my age when I was born. I asked him how he felt having a sister 13 years younger.

He said, "Interesting because you were only 5 when I went to college. So I really didn't know you very well. At least not like I knew Charlie who was only 2 years younger." He added that I was always busy being cute when he was around. He reminded me that he always brought me presents from college with STATE written on them. He said his shopping was limited to the college bookstore. He suggested I should go to STATE because I'm all set with pencils mugs and sweatshirts. I reminded him I have out grown the sweatshirts but the pencils would be nice!

For the first time I told him that I always considered myself as an only child since there was so much of an age difference between me and my brothers.

"Gee thanks!" he said, "So I guess you are pretty much a spoiled brat!"

"Mother said I could be but she has tried very hard not to let that happen."

"So has she?"

I said, "Maybe she didn't try very hard!" And he laughed.

Happy:     Brides
Sad:        Being 13 with Grandmother Liz

# FEBRUARY 13

Dear CC,

I received information today from the Department of Aging. They sent a very helpful booklet explaining Alzheimer's disease. The disease was named, in 1906, after Alois Alzheimer, a German doctor. It is a degenerative disease of the brain. Its causes are not understood and there is no cure right now. The ten warning signs of the disease were listed and Grandmother Liz has all of them. The diagnosis process is a combination of factors. Medical, psychiatric, physical, neurological, and lab tests.

Mother told me about the short memory test they gave Grandmother Liz in the doctor's office. The test was to check for possible dementia. It was back when the family first noticed strange behavior and Grandmother scored poorly. The information I got said there is no one test that determines the presence or absence of Alzheimer's disease. It is a process of elimination but the results are 90 percent accurate. There is research being done to prevent, treat and cure Alzheimer's disease. I'm pretty sure this research won't help Grandmother Liz but I hope it can help my mother's generation, mine and my nieces and nephews. I'm assuming I'll have some!

It was some comfort to read that Alzheimer's is not a normal part of aging but a disease of the brain. There are three stages of the disease: early, middle and late. Grandmother is in the middle. The late stage is when they are bed ridden, totally dependent with almost no awareness.

Even after reading the information about Alzheimer's I didn't find the answers I wanted. Why do some people get Alzheimer's and others don't? I know it's not contagious but how come my grandmother has it and someone else's grandmother doesn't? Does someone die of Alzheimer's? And does it mean my mother will get it and then me? I know the greatest risk factor is old age and Mother and I aren't there yet. But is there a test they can give us to see if we'll get it? Mother would tell me I'm worrying about this too much right now. I need to be content that Grandmother Liz is safe and receiving the best care our family can give her. Maybe over the summer I'll go to the library and read about the research part of the disease. That interests me. Maybe I can use that for a paper sometime for an assignment in high school. This may be the time I should start to think about what I want to do when I grow up. Dad used to say that Chris was a member of the "major of the month club". I can see me doing that too. I'll have to ask Chris how and when he arrived at wanting to be an attorney.

I was busy at school today helping to get the Home Ec. Fair organized that we are having next month. That will mean getting lots of cooking and sewing projects collected and ready for display. I will model the skirt and vest I made. Boys even made stuff like aprons and potholders. I don't know if they model them or not. Guys have fun with those sewing machines. I hope they don't drive cars like they run those machines!

After school LeeAnn went with me to see Grandmother Liz. She was in her room resting in her chair. I introduced LeeAnn to her and she reached for my hand like she always does. We told her about being invited to the 8$^{th}$ grade dance. I told Grandmother that LeeAnn is a good friend of mine like Molly was to her. She looked at LeeAnn when I said Molly. We talked a little longer then told her goodbye.

I thanked LeeAnn for going with me and she said she was glad she did. She said she understands my frustration at not being able to communicate with my grandmother. I told LeeAnn that I had a plan but couldn't talk about it yet. I want Grandmother to know who I am even for a few seconds.

Then I thought, "Wouldn't it be great if Molly could be here to help me with my plan?" Wonder how I could work that out?

Tomorrow night is the dance. LeeAnn asked if I could sleep over afterwards. Mother had to talk to her mother and work out the details. Whatever. Why are mothers so weird sometimes?

I'm tired and going to bed. What will I ever do with all this journal writing? I hope I see Ms. Lily sometime and tell her that I'm still trying to get her homework assignment done!

Happy:     Ms. Lily
Sad:         Department of Aging

# FEBRUARY 15

Dear CC,

WOW, what a fun night at the dance! It's 2 o'clock in the afternoon and I just got home from my sleep over at LeeAnn's. I want to write this while it is so fresh on my mind. As if I could forget it. Besides the house is quiet and it's just you and me, CC. Mom and Dad are at a Yard and Garden Show somewhere and that will take a while.

Ruben picked me up last night and gave me beautiful light pink baby roses for my wrist. I pinned a pink boutonniere on his tux. Mother had to take a ton of digital pictures and Dad used the video camera. So we were well documented. Mother wanted to print some of the good pictures so we could show our friends.

I said, "Mom, we are going to the dance and they can see us in person." Ruben just smiled. I hope he wasn't embarrassed. We left with LeeAnn, Robbie and his older brother, "The Driver."

I put an eyebrow pencil, blush and lip-gloss in the small evening bag Mother let me borrow. It was white, but served my purpose. I would need to touch up my makeup when I got to the dance. I had some on when I left but it will be more obvious after my touch up!

We went to the hall where the dance was being held. I'm so glad the dances aren't in the school gym like Chris and Charlie's were. Mother said they smelled like they'd played basketball instead of being at a dance.

I thought, "There are some similarities." The hall was decorated in our school colors, blue and silver. There were streamers and balloons everywhere. Carnations were on the tables with silver star confetti scattered on the blue tablecloths. There were snacks and punch served by parent volunteers.

A photographer took our picture under a white wooden arch. Ruben put his arm around my waist in our picture. I about melted. He looked so cool in a black tux, fancy white shirt and a big button where the tie goes. Guess that's the new version of the bow tie. Then I talked to my girl friends and Ruben went over to talk to the other guys. We talked about our dresses, our shoes, and our fancy hair-do's. The boys probably talked about our dresses, our shoes and our fancy hair-do's!

Mother took me to have my nails done but there wasn't much to work with. The pink polish is pretty. We all agreed those tuxes sure looked nice and changed our dates into "Mr. can't believe it's really you"! The D.J. started playing the music and everyone froze. It was so funny. One minute we're twirling around in our dresses and the next minute it's like "Simon says freeze"! It must have been because we thought, "What do we do now? Will the boys ask us to dance?" So a few girls started dancing by themselves and pretty soon the boys discovered us. In a short time everyone was dancing like crazy. Except for the few on the sidelines that say they can't dance and will just watch. Which meant their dates had to sit out too. Ruben asked me if I would mind if he asked Jill if she wanted to dance since her date said he wouldn't. I said sure and I'll just go over and bother her date and see if he's giving up talking too.

It seemed like the room heated up to 100 degrees after only about half an hour. The punch bowl was getting empty and the parents working the party were busy making more. Ruben and I sat down to rest and catch our breath. He said I looked very nice. I said thank you. After that last fast dance I wasn't so sure. I hoped my dress had industrial strength spaghetti straps or I'd be in a heap of trouble.

I was thinking I'm sure glad I went to the after school dance classes that the gym teacher offered. I learned a few things but also discovered if you're just fast on your feet, turn around a lot and throw your head back you're going to look like everyone else. If music is playing it's called dancing. If it's not you look pretty stupid!

It was time for Mr. and Ms. Personality to be announced. All the candidates had to go up by the picture arch and wait for the winners to be announced. I sat down with Robbie. Our 8th grade teacher sponsor read the names. Second runner up for the girls was Jenny. Then second runner up for the boys was announced. First runner up for the girls was LeeAnn. I looked at Robbie and we were both disappointed. Then first runner up for the boys was named. And finally Ms. Personality was Chelsea. Robbie and I looked at each other puzzled. Mr. Personality was Ruben. I jumped up and was so excited for him. But I was hurting for LeeAnn. Robbie and I went up to congratulate the winners and told LeeAnn how sorry we were she didn't win. We told her we couldn't believe Chelsea won. She said she couldn't either. A lot of girls were around Ruben congratulating him. I walked up and gave him a hug and said I knew he'd win. I was very happy for him. I felt so sad for my best friend.

The best part of the evening for me was the slow dances. I had learned the 1-2-3-4 square and if your date was not timid he could lead you around the room all evening doing that dance. Ruben was not timid and knew the dance too. He led and I followed. We only stepped on each other's toes a couple of times. He would squeeze my waist at the end of every dance and I thought that was so neat.

The dance ended at 10:00 and the parents practically pushed us out the door. We found "The Driver" and he took us to the "50's Place" to eat. He dropped us off and said he was meeting his girlfriend but would be back at 11:15 to take us home. Robbie told him the girls had to be home by 11:30.

LeeAnn and I didn't order our favorite hamburger because it would be too messy to eat in our formal dresses. My pink was bad enough but her dress was white and ketchup and mustard could be a real mess! So I ordered a large chocolate milk shake and French fries with melted cheese. LeeAnn ordered a large chocolate cola with vanilla ice cream and fries. The guys had the biggest hamburgers on the menu. Also the biggest fries/onion rings combo and large milk shakes. For dessert we all shared the double/trouble banana split. I probably could have eaten more but not in this dress. I had reached my limit and I really hoped my dress had not!

On the way home Ruben and I rode in the back seat. When I got in he pulled me over to the middle and told me that was a better seat belt to use than the one by the door. I'm thinking boys are amazing! We both said what a fun time we had and wished the evening wouldn't end. I told him the pink baby roses were really cool. And congratulated him again for being voted Mr. Personality. I said he really deserved it. I don't think he was listening to me because he reached over and kissed me on the lips. Again I thought I would melt or maybe even pass out. He kissed me again just to make sure it took, I guess. I hope he knew it did. We both said Happy Valentines Day at the same time. At that moment I knew what Grandmother Liz meant when she wrote in her letter that she and Molly talked about their first kiss many years later. I know I will never forget mine.

LeeAnn and I met her mom in the hall when we got to her house. The first thing LeeAnn said was she didn't win, but was first runner up.

Her mom said, "That is nice sweetheart." LeeAnn said she didn't want to talk about it right now. Her mother asked us about the dance and we told her how much fun it was and what everyone was wearing and how great the guys looked in tuxes. She started telling us about her first formal dance and I'm thinking to myself I don't really care about that right now. All I want to do is get out of this dress and think about only one thing. I excused myself and LeeAnn and her mother went into the living room to talk. I was glad her mother was up when we got home so she could talk to LeeAnn. Sometimes you just need your mom when things don't work out.

As I walked to the bedroom I heard her mom say I could fix my own breakfast when I got up. This sounded just like home. I'm not even sure if I'll be able to get to sleep much less worry about breakfast.

LeeAnn came in the bedroom about 20 minutes later and I could tell she had been crying. Again I was really glad she had her mom to talk to. I didn't even think of a situation like this when we decided to stay at her house. What would she have done if we had been at my house for our sleep over? LeeAnn and I were ready to get in bed when I saw that she had on the same pajamas that I brought. We bought them together but teased we would never wear them at the same time. She said she would change.

But I said, "Why? Who is going to see us? We can just be embarrassed between the two of us." She said okay but was probably too tired to care.

LeeAnn said she was glad she talked to her mom. Her mother agreed that losing the vote was hard especially in front of all her friends. But life goes on and she assured her daughter that she would be fine. She said it's not easy and there will be more contests in the future and this will give her experience.

Her mom also said, "One thing for sure, the sun will come up in the morning and you'll have a new day without anyone voting on it."

LeeAnn gave a sigh and turned over like she was going to sleep. I blurted out, "Did you have fun with Robbie tonight?" She said it wasn't great but okay. He said he was sorry I didn't win and that he did vote for me. I told him thank you.

Then she said, "Carly do you know what I'm really upset about tonight?"

"Because you didn't win?"

"No."

"What then?"

"Robbie didn't kiss me." I didn't know what to say. I really didn't want to share my evening right then.

I said, "I'm sorry Annie, I know you like him."

She said, "Next time I want for us to sit in the back seat. I think he didn't want 'The Driver' to see him. He would probably tease him and tell his friends. Well, it was either Robbie's brother or a parent." She said her Dad could have driven their van and we all could have been in a back seat. "Maybe we should have let the boys get a limo after all."

I was afraid she was going to ask me about Ruben so I said, "We better get to sleep; my feet are killing me." She said good night and thanked me for being her best friend. I told her she didn't have to thank me and we'll always be best friends.

I said, "Annie, did you vote for yourself?"

"No."

"You should have!" I heard a giggle. I think Annie is my Molly.

Happy:     Ruben
Sad:       Disappointment

# MARCH 14

Dear CC,

Yesterday afternoon Mother and I went to another wedding shower for Abby. It wasn't as much fun as the first one. Not all her bridesmaids could go and it was mostly Mother's friends. It was at my aunt's house about 30 miles away. She is my Dad's younger sister and we don't see her family very often. I call my aunt "Weird Wanda" and my cousin just "Weird." That isn't fair. Her name is Tamara and we get along fine. She is 2 years older than I am but she looks 10 years older. She dyes her hair jet black, wears black makeup and all black clothes. She'll fit right in at the wedding. She also has several tattoos, which pretty much turns me off. Except that I would really like a tiny rose tattoo on my ankle. "Weird" would never notice. But it's going to be hard to convince Mom. I'll be well along in high school before that subject ever comes up.

The shower was another fun time for Abby. Chris had told her all about his relatives and Mom's friends so she knew where everyone lived, worked and what to ask about. She even knew the names of their children. She really impressed me with her family knowledge. Way to go Abby! That was certainly a good way to win acceptance into the family. Aunt Wanda loved her and wanted to know everything about the wedding. Abby was such a good sport and spent a lot of time talking to her. Abby's interest in everyone was amazing. I'm sure Mother was proud of her daughter-in-law to be.

Abby got more great gifts. She must have every kitchen gadget there is. I didn't even know what some of them were for. Tamara and her sister gave Abby a stainless steel waste can for the kitchen. That was the good part. In it they put a lot of canned goods for the kitchen cabinets. The catch was they had torn the labels off. That should make for some interesting meals. I knew there was a reason I called my cousin "Weird".

Mondays at school are always fun talking about our weekend. This one was especially fun because they had our dance pictures for sale. Ruben and I both bought ours. Everyone shared pictures but not in classes.

The teachers said, "No pictures out of book bags." That was probably a good idea or I would have just stared at mine. I like Ruben a lot. But high school is only months away and I can imagine more freshman girls than just me will think he's cute and very nice. I'll just enjoy 8th grade while I can.

I was walking to math class with LeeAnn and she said, "Carly, you never told me about your date with Ruben."

"We had a good time and he's a great dancer."

She asked, "How about as a kisser?" I know I blushed.

"That too."

"She smiled and said, "I thought so. I figured you didn't want to talk about it at my house." She said that she was so glad we had a sleep over after the dance. I am too.

Eighth grade classes had an assembly today to give honors and recognition to the outstanding students. It was both for grades and participation in school activities. My name was on both lists and I was pleased. Recognition was given to the students who raised their grades the most during the year. I was really glad to hear their names because those students aren't the ones that everyone knows but the ones that struggle to stay in school. It's important that their work be recognized. There were 16 students who received gift certificates to the mall for perfect attendance. I think that is amazing. They are either very healthy or their mothers don't put them through a health checklist every morning. The class officers were thanked. All the club officers were named and the Volunteer Club members were thanked for starting their club this year. Our principal said it made a positive contribution to our community.

The principal asked Ruben and Chelsea to come up to the stage. Everyone clapped really loud, which said they were certainly the popular choices. I looked over at LeeAnn and she just rolled her eyes. I felt sorry for her all over again. Ruben and Chelsea received certificates. The assembly closed with several announcements. Next week all 8th graders that will attend Center High School next fall will spend all day Tuesday at the school. We will eat in the lunchroom and sit in on classes. It sounds fun and scary. I feel so secure right now I'm sure high school will be a big adjustment and be a big change in my small comfortable world. And I thought 6th graders were babies! Hope I'm ready.

Tonight was the Home Economics Fair. Lots of food and a fashion show for all the things made in Sewing I and II. I modeled my skirt. It was cut on the bias, had several panels and was complicated to make. You couldn't see all the sweat I put into it for just a B+. I also made a matching vest. I got an A+ on it without all the sweat. Go figure. The outfit pretty much averaged out to an A project!

The boys didn't even argue when Ms. Taylor asked them to model their aprons, oven mitts and even chef hats. They were a riot. Ruben made a red apron with "GUSTO" appliquéd on it in red gingham. I thought, "Way to go Ruben. No wonder you get A's in Sewing I."

Happy:     Eighth Grade
Sad:       Leaving Eighth Grade

# APRIL 10

Dear CC,

There are six more weeks of school. I can't believe this school year is almost over. It has been the best year for me for a lot of reasons. I have really liked 8th grade. I learned a lot and I feel like I grew up a lot. I enjoyed all my after school activities, especially the Volunteer Club. It didn't hurt to have Ruben for a boy friend! He is very sweet and I've enjoyed our time together. He was involved in school like I was so he didn't have time to want me to do something with him all the time and then be mad if I didn't. Clarissa has a boyfriend like that and she didn't belong to any out of school activities because Kenny would have a fit, pout and act like a baby. That is not the kind of boyfriend I want.

The other event that was so important to me this year was Grandmother Liz' letter. I never expected anything like that. And if I hadn't gotten it I know I would never have tried to communicate with her. Up until I was 13 I never saw her more than once or twice a month and never talked to her because she didn't respond and I thought it didn't make any difference. Mother never pushed me to do any differently, which I appreciated. I still think she feels badly for me and probably thinks it is too painful for me to be with

Grandmother. The best memories of my grandmother stopped when I was 5 or 6. Before Grandmother got sick. At that age I didn't have many conversations with her. Certainly not about the things she mentioned in her letter. I don't want to have to settle for that. My plan has to work. I still want Grandmother Liz to know me as her only granddaughter that loves her very much. I think of all the times she reaches for my hand and touches my birthstone ring. I feel she is trying to communicate.

Then I think of all the times Ruben and I hold hands and I wonder what that means. I think it is similar, but different. He and I like each other and enjoy being together and that is how we show it. I would love for Grandmother to meet Ruben but that is completely out of the realm of possibility. That is another reason why Alzheimer's frustrates me. I'm going to wait until after Chris and Abby's wedding before I carry out my plan with Grandmother Liz.

We had our final Volunteer meeting after school today. There are several 6th and 7th graders in it so the 8th graders feel like the club will be continued next year. I hope so because it is important both for the students and for the people they reach out to.

We did our reporting on our hours. A.J. volunteered to start an after school basketball game for the young boys in his neighborhood. He was sure he had more fun then they did. Bobby reported two hours of helping a disabled 3rd grader read. He said he was really a sweet kid and plans to continue meeting with him during the summer at his day care center. I think we all saw again that we get as much out of volunteering as the people we spend time with.

There were forty-three hours reported this two week period. Everyone has really gotten involved. LeeAnn read from another cookbook to Mrs. Bryant. LeeAnn said she would continue this summer and Mrs. Bryant wants her to read from a seed catalog about all the pretty flowers. We all agreed that would be interesting.

At breakfast this morning I asked Mother what was in the box in the attic with "Liz" written on it. She said it was Grandmother Liz' things that were moved out of her apartment when she went to the nursing home. I immediately said, "I want to go through it." Mom said she didn't remember what was saved but mostly small keepsakes that my children might like having some day that belonged to their great grandmother. I said I couldn't wait that long! I asked Mom to ask Dad if he would put it in my room for me. Mother said words like bugs, dirt and musty.

I said, "Bugs, dirt and musty don't bother me. I have a plan and that box might be of some help."

"A plan?"

"Yes, but I can't talk about it yet." Dad came in the kitchen and I asked him to put the box in the attic with "Liz" on it in my room. He said okay. Only mothers worry about bugs and stuff. It was much easier asking Dad myself.

Happy:     Volunteering
Sad:        Middle School Ending

# APRIL 30

Dear CC,

After school today I opened the box and it smelled like the attic. What I found was Grandmother's life before her illness. It was so strange. Things she talked about in her letter, things Mother has told me about and mementoes that had Grandmother Liz written all over them. I got tears in my eyes because I knew that they had no meaning to my Grandmother now but at one time they were very important to her—they were her life. The life she can't remember. I started taking the things out carefully like they were worth millions. After all I was holding her life treasures.

On top was a small hat with a veil. A piece of paper pinned to the inside said, "Worn on my wedding day". Oh my gosh! There were embroidered dishtowels and pillowcases. A small book titled "Afternoon Tea for Discerning Ladies". Whatever that means! I opened it and Molly had written, "To my best friend for all our past and future teas. Love, Molly."

What was missing in this box is what Grandmother could tell me about each item. The stories would be priceless. I thought, "I can't get discouraged. I have to settle for what I have found." Then I saw the first item for my plan. Two aprons. One said, "Grandmother," the other, "Grandmother's Little Helper". These were the ones in the picture in my album. Hers was clean. Mine had all the stains of everything I ever helped her make. I found more pictures to add to the album Mother made for me. I found a book with a satin cover that said "Our Wedding". It had Molly's signature as maid of honor like Grandmother said in her letter. I found a small baby doll. It looked like it had a rough life. It was soft, dirty and probably loved a lot by someone. Me, I hope. I'll have to ask Mother about it. At the bottom was a thick cookbook, no pictures just recipes. The hard cover was falling off and it had lots of stains like my apron. Mother told me once that Grandmother always knew where to find her favorite recipes. They are in the book with the most stains, turned back pages and pieces of newspaper used for a bookmark. I wonder if I have to learn these things to be able to get married or does it just suddenly come to you when you say, "I do"? I wonder if Abby knows about this? I don't think so. She got a wall hanging at her shower that said, "Dinner Ordered—Carry Out 20 Minutes". Everyone laughed but Abby. So what will she do with those beautiful fancy cookbooks?

It looked like Mother had dumped a desk drawer in the box. Lots of little stuff like pins, paper clips, pencils, thread on wooden spools. What is that about? There were lots of keys. I didn't have time to imagine what those belonged to. But I bet Grandmother Liz knew. The next thing I found was a small thick dark brown book with a very faded "My Diary" on the front. A small strap held it closed and locked. It smelled very musty. Mother knew what she was talking about. Oh my gosh, that was too much, CC. She even kept a diary like my journal. I knew I had found something so personal and special I could not even open it. That is for my children or better yet my grandchildren. Besides it was locked and I didn't even try to find the key in the mess in the bottom of the box. One other thing I found that might help my plan was a big silver colored pin. I think Mother would call it a brooch. I have to admit it was pretty ugly. But I'm not to judge. I put that with the aprons and recipe book. I found a pair of white leather gloves in size tiny. I've never seen gloves like that before. I like my thermal ones better. There were several lace handkerchiefs. One of these would be good for the plan. There were lots of pages of paper that looked like articles but I didn't throw them away. Those were to read another time. There was a strange looking wooden box shaped like a triangle sitting in the bottom of the box. There was a piece of paper under it that said "Aunt May's metronome". I had no idea what it was. I never heard of a metronome and who was Aunt May? Another question for Mother. I put everything back in the box, except what I needed. I closed the lid and pushed it in a corner of my room where I wanted to keep it for a while. I just remembered I didn't see Grandmother's wedding pictures. Another question to ask.

I went back to the attic to look for a small box to put my things in for the plan. I thought I was seeing a ghost. A plain white face with blond hair was staring at me. After I cleared the lump in my throat I realized it was a wig on a stand. I'll be asking Mother about that too. I found the box I needed. I always had in mind that keepsakes were kept in a trunk or some place that had some special meaning. But

Grandmother Liz' keepsakes are in a big dirty smelly cardboard box and she doesn't even know it.

Today was boring at school. I've decided I'm ready for high school. It wasn't completely boring because I talked to Ruben.


Happy:    Keepsakes
Sad:      Unknown Memories

# MAY 10

Dear CC,

Today a bus picked us up at school and took us to high school for the day. Ruben sat next to me and we talked about leaving middle school and becoming freshmen. I admitted I was a little nervous and he said he was too. I thought that was cool that a guy would admit that and especially to a girl. He said he wanted to go out for sports but didn't know how that would go. I told him I was excited about the classes I wanted to take and the after school activities I could get involved in. I said I bet it will be a lot different than 8th grade. Ruben said at least they have lockers like we're used to so we can look cool between classes. He reached for my hand, squeezed it, and smiled.

It was a fun day touring the school. The building is huge and looked like it will be easy to get lost in. I really liked the fact that freshmen were in charge of the tours. They shared their experiences hoping that we could avoid the bad ones.

Our guide, Sara, said, "Don't fall for anything an upper classman tells you about stairs, doors or teachers. They are supposed to be good examples and be helpful and most are. Some will try to reduce you to tears. Remember that the building has only three floors, so don't go up that half flight of stairs at the center of the hall on the third floor. You'll be coming right back down and there will probably be a bunch of laughing students waiting for you. That's when you will want to crawl in your book bag!"

We had a choice of which classes we wanted to visit. I chose algebra, home ec., and Spanish. I also want to take chorus and art but I could only pick three classes to visit today. Those are three I want to enroll in my first year. I thought the teachers were just like middle school. You can tell their personality right away and you know whether they are tolerable to a point or there is no second chance with them. I really liked the Spanish teacher, I felt like I'd have a second chance with her!

LeeAnn, Robbie, Ruben and I ate lunch together in the lunchroom. That experience was nothing like middle school. It will take a year for me to figure that out. There are ten times more choices of food, and more lines to pay. Then figure out where to sit. I hope someone I know is in my lunch period or I'll look like a freshman for sure.

Ruben said he visited with the coaches and got information about tryouts for teams and everything required to do that. He seemed excited about the possibility of playing football and/or basketball. He also visited a science and an algebra class. I noticed when I was walking with him that girls he didn't know came up to him to say hi. That is only the beginning, I'm sure. It makes me wonder if I'll see him or even hear from him this summer. Time will tell.

On the way back on the bus the four of us decided to get together again and go out to eat at the "50's Place" and go to a movie. I said we could call it the end of middle school celebration and they agreed. LeeAnn immediately said her Dad could drive. She didn't look at me but I smiled anyway.

When I got home Mother wanted to know all about high school and I shared it all with her. She said I sounded excited and I agreed that I was. I said I had four questions for her.

She said, "Oh Dear!"

"Whose baby doll is that in Grandmother Liz' box?"

She said, "It was yours and when you were through playing with it, Grandmother said she'd like to keep it since it belonged to her only granddaughter."

"I want to keep it in my room now." She said that would be fine.

Next question was, "Mother did you ever wear a wig?"

"Oh no, you found some pictures I thought I had thrown away."

"No, I found the wig."

"Really?" I told her that when I was looking in the attic for a small box for my plan, I happened to look over in the corner and saw this white face with long blond hair and a piece of tissue draped over it. It scared me at first because I couldn't figure out what it was. Then I realized it was a Styrofoam head with a wig on top.

Mother was a little flustered but explained wigs were "in" when Charlie and Chris were little and she and her friends all bought one and wore them only a couple of times.

I said, "So a fad that you didn't like very much."

"Yes."

"Kind of like LeeAnn and I when we got our ears pierced except we liked it."

"Well not exactly like that," she said. Maybe Mother hoped we wouldn't like pierced ears but it didn't work out that way. I'm waiting until high school to mention the word tattoo! I told Mother I wish I had found the wig and stand several years ago and would have used it for my scary stories at my sleep overs.

"You don't tell scary stories anymore?"

I said, "MOTHER, we talk about boys now!"

"Well that can be scary too." I didn't tell her, but I agree.

"Third question. What is a metronome?"

"Are you finally going to start piano lessons?"

"What does that have to do with my question?" She said a metronome is an instrument for making exact time by a regularly repeated tick: It helps you keep time while playing a piano.

"How come I had never heard of it?"

"Probably because you've never taken piano lessons." She had to admit she hasn't seen one in a really long time either. Then I asked who Aunt May was. She said she was a cousin of Grandmother Liz' who never married so Grandmother included her in our family while Mother was growing up. Everyone called her Aunt May even though she wasn't our aunt. I said that sounds like something Grandmother Liz would have done. What a sweet lady.

"Fourth question. What happened to Grandmother's wedding pictures?" Mother thought maybe they were in another box of our family pictures in the attic. She said we'd look for them sometime. I wondered when that would be. Mother said that I have found some pretty interesting things in that box.

"I hope I have. I'll find out soon."

I'm tired tonight. Center High School wore me out and I haven't even started yet. But I am excited about being a freshman. I wonder if I will still be Ruben's girl friend.

Happy:     Center High School
Sad:       The unknown

# MAY 26

Dear CC,

I have been so busy I haven't even had time to write in my journal. You are probably wondering what happened to me CC. I'm still here but the end of school was fun and sad at the same time. The most fun time was going with Ruben to dinner and a movie. LeeAnn's father did drive and she and Robbie got in the farthest back seat and Ruben and I were in the first back seat. LeeAnn didn't tell me details but things must have gone the way she wanted because she said Robbie is the greatest and she hopes they continue to go out. I'm glad the kissing issue got worked out. I have no complaints!

Tomorrow Mother and I host the afternoon tea for Abby, her mother, grandmother and bridesmaids and the females in our family. Mother said my hot pink dress was too formal, like I thought, so I got to get a short dressy dress. It is black and white and more cute than pretty I thought. But it did fit in with the wedding theme.

We had table favors for each guest and spent way too much time on getting those ready. They are little silver boxes with a metal bow on top of the lid. We put candy kisses in them. We stuck the guests' name cards in the bows so we assigned the seats. Hey,

71

we're the hosts and can do what we want! Mother is more nervous about this than I am. It's just a tea. How hard can it be?

I went to see Grandmother Liz this afternoon. I wish she could go to the tea but I know that wouldn't be possible. Abby and Chris wanted to invite her to the wedding too. The nurses thought it would be too confusing for her to be away from the nursing home for that big of an occasion. My mother would be the person she would have to sit with and Mom has other responsibilities. Anyway I visited her and told her about the wedding and about the end of my 8th grade. She just held my hands and looked at me. Today I felt so sorry for her because she is missing out sharing with her family. I know she doesn't know the difference, but I do. And it's sad. I told her I loved her and would be back again. She looked sad when I left. Some days I can't keep from crying and today was one of those days. I was really upset with Alzheimer's today.

When I got home from seeing Grandmother Liz I noticed her keepsake box was gone from my room. I ran to the attic and there it was. I figured the bugs and dirt were getting to Mother so she had Dad take it back. Well they don't bother me so I'll ask Dad to return it to my room. I want to be in charge of the box for now. Mother must not have wanted it in my room for my company tonight. It would make her look bad.

I invited Marie over to dinner. We fixed pizza and we ate in my bedroom. She wanted to talk about high school and about this summer. She helps take care of her brothers and sisters during the summer so she doesn't have a lot of time to do things for herself. We decided that we'd try to get together with LeeAnn and Clarissa one evening a week during the summer. Marie said she would set up a time to have it at her house after my brother's wedding and call

LeeAnn and Clarissa. I'm glad we're all staying in touch. We'll need each other for sure when school starts.

Our friend Missy moved away after school was out. I would hate to move just before high school. You wouldn't have any friends for sure. At least I'll be in the same building with my 8th grade friends; whether I ever see them or not is another question.

I'm continuing my volunteering this summer just because I enjoy visiting with the people at the nursing home. The hours won't count except for my own satisfaction. And that counts for something!

Happy:     Summer
Sad:        Alzheimer's

# MAY 31

Dear CC,

The tea was a success. Abby and her mother were very happy that we had it and thanked us a lot. Too much, I thought. Abby looked very pretty in a short white summer dress that looked great with her wonderful tan. She will be a beautiful bride. Everyone loved the little silver box favors. I told Mother our work was worth it.

We all introduced ourselves and told how we knew Abby and some told funny stories. Abby's good friend, Holly, had the best stories because she had known her since grade school. They also went to high school together. There was lots of laughing and picture taking. It wasn't stuffy and quiet like I thought a tea would be. Maybe it should have been but ours wasn't. I probably should have checked out the book about teas I found in Grandmother Liz' keepsake box. Tamara even seemed to have a good time. She wore a long black skirt and white lacey blouse. She could be the mascot for the wedding with her black and white outfits! I think our waitresses even enjoyed it. They kept bringing the fancy food and tea pots. When Mother showed me the bill I thought maybe we had too much fun! Mom was cool and I knew she enjoyed it as much as I did.

Tomorrow night is the rehearsal dinner that Mom and Dad are in charge of. They are having it at a local restaurant that has a party room in the back. Mother has worried about the menu for days. We even went over to sample the food at lunch recently. I think Mom wished she had taken someone else because I thought everything was delicious. We went to the restaurant today to decorate the room. The room was available a day ahead and that was good. Mother will probably stress out anyway.

After the dinner there will be a wedding rehearsal. I think Abby's mother is in charge of that. At least Mother said she didn't have to worry about it. I can't imagine 14 attendants plus me up in front with Chris and Abby. It could be a zoo, but I hope not.

Ruben called me tonight to say hi and ask how my summer was going. I said it hadn't started yet but will soon after my brother's wedding. He laughed and said he missed seeing me at school every day. I blushed and said in two and a half months we'd be back in school and I hoped I would see him in that big building we're going to. He said we'd have to plan a place where we could meet between classes. He's assuming I'll be organized enough to do that. Maybe we'll be lucky enough to have the same lunch period. He said he was busy working for his Dad and liked earning the extra money.

I said, "I'm still on the allowance payroll!" I thanked him for calling and he said we would talk again soon. I said that would be great. I can't believe I'll be going to high school and he'll still be my boyfriend. That would be so awesome but just wonder if it will really happen.

I need to go to bed and rest up for the next two days. I'm excited for my brother. I think he will make a great husband just like he has been a brother. And I'll get another sister-in-law out of the deal. I get along with Charlie's wife fine but don't see her very often. I hope Abby likes to be around me or maybe I'm too young for her to spend any time with. It will be interesting since they live close to us in Aurora.

Happy:    Celebrations
Sad:      Stress

# JUNE 12

Dear CC,

Oh my Gosh. It's all over. My brother is married. It's been almost 2 weeks but seems like just yesterday.

I'll start with the rehearsal dinner. It went perfect, at least almost. They had places set for 25. Mother had called in to change it to 32 and the right person didn't get the message. So Mother was embarrassed and upset for a few minutes but she got over it. The bridesmaids got to bring boyfriends or husbands and that was a last minute change Abby made.

Abby's grandmother was there and she said a lot of nice things about Abby and Chris. They visit her often and she told how much she appreciated that. Of course I was wishing Grandmother Liz could have been there to say the same thing about my brother and Abby. She would have loved this wedding and all the events that have taken place. Especially the tea. My anger for her disease comes out when I'm not expecting it as it did that day.

There were lots of toasts and lots of laughing. My brother has some cool friends and they all seem to enjoy each other a lot. By having seven groomsmen he has been, and will be, in lots of their weddings. Sounds expensive to me.

Abby handed out gifts to all the girls in the wedding, even the mothers. She gave the bridesmaids pearl earrings and a pearl bracelet to wear at the wedding. She gave me a smaller pair of pearl earrings and a beautiful white frame for their wedding picture. My birthstone ring goes perfect with the jewelry. The mothers got a beautiful large white album with Chris and Abby's names printed on the front for wedding pictures. They seemed to really appreciate them. I wonder who pays for the pictures that go in them?

Chris gave the groomsmen black onyx buttons to wear on their shirts instead of ties. They came in a cute wooden box. I looked around afterwards to see if any of the guys left the boxes but no one did. I was liking that box a lot! Chris also gave them a monogrammed silver belt buckle with the date of his wedding engraved on the back. Wonder if Abby helped him with that or if it was his idea? Pretty cool I thought.

Chris stayed at our house for the night and Abby stayed with her parents at the motel. How weird. But they didn't want to see each other until the wedding. I had some time to hang out with Chris after Mom and Dad went to bed. I asked him if he was nervous and he said not really. He said he'd known Abby for so long and was so comfortable around her there was no reason to be nervous. I wondered about Abby.

I asked Chris about why he wanted to be a lawyer. And when did he decide? He laughed and said he wished he knew. It just seemed like the thing to do. After he finished college he didn't know what area he wanted to get a job in, so law school sounded like a good idea. He said he majored in business and that might fit into an attorney's job. So it all just kind of came together. I'm glad he didn't tell me it was just because he liked to argue! He said when he was my age he didn't think about being an attorney. He told me if I knew what I want to be, now wasn't too soon to start. He said my summer jobs and internships could be in that area. I said I had no idea what I wanted to do. He reminded me I had lots of time to decide.

Chris gave me a big hug before I went to bed. He said he hoped that I would come visit him and Abby. He assured me Abby didn't think I was a stupid little sister. He said Abby would like to take me shopping or out to eat sometime. They don't live that far from us and I would love to do that. I told Chris to sleep well and I hoped he enjoyed his wedding day. He smiled and said he was planning on it. It's nice to have older brothers.

As he was walking away he said, "Oh, I forgot something. I forgot to tell you that we invited someone to the wedding that I know you will want to meet. I couldn't imagine who that could be until he said, "Molly." He said he and Abby wanted Grandmother Liz to be at the wedding but since she couldn't they would invite her best friend. Molly wrote Abby a note and said she would love to come and was planning to stay with her own granddaughter for an extended visit this summer. Her granddaughter, Marsha, lives close to us. All kinds of questions started going through my head. I couldn't wait to meet Molly. I wonder if she would be interested in helping me with my plan to help me communicate with Grandmother Liz. I've already decided I'll ask her.

Chris gave me another hug and said, "Little sisters are special."

The wedding day was very busy and lots of fun. There was an early morning rain that made the outside look and smell clean. Then the sun came out and it was a beautiful day. Chris liked the rain. He said it saved him from hosing down the deck and driveway. So with his extra time Mother gave him another job: take the cars to the car wash and fill them up with gas. He thought maybe hosing down the deck would have been easier—and cheaper.

There were lots of relatives in and out of our house. Mother called it a three ring circus and I just called it family. Everyone wanted a picture with Chris while he was still a bachelor. Charlie gave Chris a hard time about giving up his freedom and was saying funny things about married life. My sister-in-law Claire just smiled and said Charlie really has it rough! Claire fit into our family immediately with a name that started with a "C". Abby is an outsider but we love her anyway. Chris said he just never met a girl with a "C" name that he liked. We were glad he quit looking.

During lunch Claire asked if I would sit with her on the deck. She didn't know all of Chris' friends so said she just wanted to be with family. Sometime during dessert she told me she had a secret to tell me. Before I could guess she told me I was going to be an aunt. Then she said I was the only one she has told and not to say anything yet. I was ready to yell but immediately closed my mouth and promised I wouldn't tell. She said Charlie didn't want to take away from Chris' wedding so he plans to tell our parents after Chris and Abby leave tonight. I am so excited.

After lunch everyone grabbed what they needed for the wedding and we left. Mother was hoping no one forgot anything.

We got dressed in a very nice dressing room with lots of mirrors and lots of room. We needed the room for Abby and seven bridesmaids. Abby's dress was beautiful. It had a long white skirt with a short train and separate sleeveless top. The white satin was plain except for tiny pearls sewed on the top and the skirt. Her veil was waist length and held on with a small crown of pearls. When no one was around Abby, I went up to her and whispered that I wanted to wear her dress when I got married. She hugged me and said she would save it for me. Her bridesmaids learned how to pull up the train and fasten it after the ceremony. I was amazed that those dresses come with directions!

We all had on the jewelry Abby had given us. I looked at my birthstone ring and thought of Grandmother Liz and how perfect it was for my brother's wedding. Our flowers arrived and mine was a wrist corsage like Ruben gave me. Instead of pink roses mine was one small orchid. I liked the roses better. The photographer took a ton of pictures in the dressing rooms. That should have prepared me for all the pictures after the ceremony. But nothing had prepared me for that.

I was wondering if the photographer was using color film. She could have used black and white. Then I realized she probably wasn't using film at all. I haven't gotten a digital camera yet. I thought I might get one for graduating from 8th grade but Mom and Dad thought I needed luggage instead. Then they told me that was for our vacation to Disney World this summer. So not a bad deal after all.

It was time for the ceremony and everyone was getting nervous. We heard the music and it was exciting. I went down the aisle after the bridesmaids and just before Abby. I got to stand by the maid of honor and hold the bride's bouquet when the wedding rings were exchanged. I watched my brother's face when Abby started down the aisle and he looked amazed. I guess it was a good idea that he hadn't seen Abby all day and had never seen the dress. He may not have been nervous but he looked a little shocked at how beautiful Abby looked. I've heard people say that all brides are beautiful and Abby certainly was. I have my doubts about a couple of girls I know being beautiful brides. Anyway, the ceremony was perfect and Mom and Sue did not mess up lighting the unity candle. Mother was nervous but it didn't show. When Abby and Chris turned around after the ceremony to walk back down the aisle they stopped and kissed both mothers. It was so sweet I couldn't help but cry.

After the ceremony Mother introduced me to Molly and her granddaughter Marsha. Marsha is Charlie's age. I had so much to say I almost forgot to say, "I'm so glad to meet you."

Finally I said, "I would like to visit with you at the reception."

Molly said, "I would like that too." So now my plan is coming alive.

Next more pictures and then the reception. I think my favorite picture will be me with Chris. I will also like the one taken with Claire and Charlie. I hope I didn't give away their secret by smiling so much.

After the pictures I had my first limo ride. It was really fun. I sat back and thought about Ruben being there with me. I snapped out of that and had a cola and enjoyed the ride and all the noise. The bridal party had been too quiet and too good for too long. It's like when I was little. Mom used to tell me when I was bad, that I was tired of being good for so long. It was like that in the limo. Chris and Abby were with us. I wondered what the other limo was like without the bride and groom!

The reception was a really big party. Lots of food, music and dancing. It would have been more fun if Ruben had been there. I wanted LeeAnn to come but Mother said I couldn't ask her. Wonder what wedding law that comes under? I had fun anyway. There were some guests my age and they asked me to dance. They were not as good dancers as Ruben. We stumbled over each other but were polite.

I spent time talking to Molly. She asked lots of questions about Grandmother Liz. I told her about getting her letter on my birthday. I told her about my visits and what I was trying to do. I want Grandmother Liz to know who I am and to know how much I loved her letter. Molly looked at Marsha and they smiled. Then Molly said she and Grandmother Liz had decided when they were teenagers that if they had children and then granddaughters they wanted to write them letters and share some things about themselves. Molly had the first granddaughter. But after two grandsons Grandmother Liz didn't know if she was going to be able to write her letter. So my birth was very special and that's why Grandmother wrote that she had been thinking about the letter for a long time. Molly said the one thing they didn't consider was their health in 50 or 60 years. She said dementia was not something they even thought about, much less Alzheimer's. It was a word that was seldom used. Molly said they just knew they would be old and laughed about that.

I asked why they decided to write letters to granddaughters and not grandsons. Molly said because girls like to share similar things that wouldn't be interesting to boys. Molly had three granddaughters so she got to write three letters. Marsha said she was glad her grandmother and Liz had decided that because her letter has meant so much to her. Marsha said she has always been amazed that two young girls would think of something like that that would have such long term meaning. I agreed. I began wondering what amazing thing LeeAnn and I could come up with. We would never have thought of Molly and Grandmother's idea. What teenager thinks about being a grandmother?

Then I asked Molly if she would go with me to see Grandmother Liz. She said of course. She knew that Grandmother Liz wasn't doing well with Alzheimer's and she wanted to see her. I told her about my plan and she said she would help me any way she could. I thanked her and said I would call her in a few days and we could go to the nursing home. I invited Marsha but she declined. She said that was a time for just the three of us. I was thinking her being there would be nice but she was right and I appreciated it. Now my plan is ready to go.

I saw Tamara sitting by herself and went over to talk to her. She had on a long black dress with an off white cape. I'll have to say it was very striking. She certainly didn't look 15. She asked me if I was scared of going to high school. I said I hope I won't be scared. I was thinking more like just being nervous. She said she was scared most of her freshman year. I asked why. She said she didn't have any friends and other students made fun of her because of the way she dressed. She said they called her names and made her very uncomfortable. I asked if she talked to anyone about it. She said she finally talked to a school counselor who suggested she make a big effort to make friends and to ignore the name calling, as hard as that would be. I asked if it worked. She said yes, but both requests were hard to do. She said she now has two good friends and tries not to dress so extreme at school and save that for the weekends. For the first time she's looking forward to the new school year. She thinks being a junior will be cool. I asked her if she had a boyfriend and she said boys were not on her radar right now. I was just wondering if Ruben would like her. She asked me if a friend and I would like to go to a movie with her and her friends sometime. I said that would be fun. I'll have to keep that in mind. I haven't been in a car yet with a 16 year old driver, so I have a feeling that would get a no from Mom and Dad. My argument would be, "But she's family!" Actually I'm not real comfortable with that idea myself right now. But I was glad she asked and I thanked her.

Next was the bride throwing the bouquet. Abby told me she was going to throw it to me. She said she didn't want to make her bridesmaids mad. So I stood in front of everyone and caught it. It didn't matter that the bridesmaids were all mad at me. Everyone clapped. Now what will I do with a wedding bouquet for the next 20 years? Mother teased me about catching the bouquet. She said I don't have to decide any time soon about getting married. She hoped I wouldn't have 7 bridesmaids when I do. I said I would try to stay in the 2 or 3 range. We both laughed about our silly conversation.

When Abby and Chris left after the reception we all threw flower petals. Petals didn't hurt them or the environment. I had been concerned about that and told Chris he couldn't have anything that would harm anything or anybody. He just gave a big brother smile. I want rose petals thrown when I get married. Pink.

Mom, Dad and I were some of the last to leave the reception. We were all exhausted. Our drive home was quiet. I did say I thought the wedding was beautiful and I was so happy for Chris and Abby. I was thinking that I hoped I looked that happy when I get married, if I do. Then I told Mom I wanted some more cake. Dad got interested in that idea. When we got home we went to the kitchen, kicked off our shoes, and started cutting some of the cake Sue had asked us to take home. We even got out ice cream and Dad made some coffee. Another party was starting. And it was a good thing because I knew Charlie and Claire would be at our house shortly.

Two hours later we were stuffed again and celebrating a whole different event. It was such a cool time for Charlie and Claire. They said they didn't have a big wedding so tonight was a little bittersweet for them. But the baby announcement was a first for our family so I think they felt pretty special. I think Claire shared every day since the day they found out they were having a baby. I wanted to know if the baby was a boy or girl but they said they didn't want to know. Charlie said he always loved surprises and besides he didn't care. To have a healthy baby was all he and Claire wanted. I was so happy for them. Mom and Dad were too. Dad said he couldn't wait to be married to a grandmother. I thought, "Dad, don't get weird on us." You never know what parents are going to say.

Today has been overwhelming. I didn't know that there could be so much happiness to share with family in one day. I was afraid the bubble would burst or something bad would happen. I knew then that I needed sleep. I was beginning not to think straight. I told everyone good night and stumbled into bed. I had about 30 seconds to think about Ruben before I was asleep. Charlie and Claire were staying over a couple more days before flying home. Maybe Claire and I could go shopping for baby things before they leave.

Happy:     Brothers
Sad:       Grandmother Liz

# JUNE 18

Dear CC,

After school was out and the wedding was over I moved at a much slower pace. Now I go to the pool a couple of times a week. I do some babysitting for our neighbor down the street. But not for free! They should pay me double for their obnoxious kids. I stopped by to see Mrs. Horton with the two broken arms. She had already gone home. I read a lot and really enjoy that. I walk to the library and usually meet LeeAnn there and we talk on the patio about Robbie and Ruben. We both have no idea if they will even know us when school starts. High school friends tell us we should forget them now before they dump us. They said freshman boys are the worst. Their egos are too big to be around freshman girls. They will only look at sophomore girls. I think the best thing for LeeAnn and me is to quit listening to high school girls.

Before Charlie and Claire went home she, Mother, and I went shopping for baby things. It was so fun seeing my sister-in-law so excited about her baby. She bought blankets, crib sheets and things she needed that didn't matter if it was a boy or girl. Everything she got was white, yellow or mint green. I bought the baby's first teddy bear. Claire was so excited she almost cried. It was a fun time and I'm glad we got to share it with her. She said her friends were having a shower for her in a few months and hoped Mother and I could come. I said I hoped so too. I could introduce myself as the aunt-to-be. Cool.

Another big event this summer was my birthday, June 8th. Being 14 was a lot less stressful than last year and 13. But that was fine with me. Mom and Dad gave me a gift card to buy clothes for our trip to Disney World. They also said I could invite Ruben, LeeAnn and Robbie and they would take us to whatever restaurant we wanted to eat at, then pick us up later. I thought that was a nice gift from my parents. They recognize I have a boyfriend and that we'd like to go out without parents. LeeAnn and I decided we liked the "50's Place" better than the guys so we picked our second best place. We went to "Pizza Platter". They have good music too and it's a fun place. Several high school students were there so we felt like we were part of the crowd. Most of our talk was about high school. We are all excited for school to start. Robbie was kind of quiet and didn't talk as much about school as the rest of us. Of course that made LeeAnn nervous. I told her not to imagine anything and just enjoy the evening. I'll probably have to eat my big brave words because we're both thinking the same thing.

Ruben and LeeAnn had birthday presents for me. Ruben gave me a CD of my favorite female singer. I was so impressed. LeeAnn gave me a book that we had talked about at the library. She thought I should have my own copy. How cool for her to think of that.

Robbie said, "Happy Birthday, could I buy you another cola?" At least Robbie hasn't lost his sense of humor.

LeeAnn said she had arranged for her mom to pick us up and go to her house to listen to CD's. I said I'd call my parents to tell them they don't have to come get us. LeeAnn said they already know. I said cool. I was thinking, "The gifts keep coming." So LeeAnn called her mom. Guess who beat Ruben and me to the furthest back seat? But that doesn't make any difference to Ruben!

I was wishing I had known we were going to LeeAnn's and I would have brought some of my CD's. But LeeAnn had already thought of that and had my mother bring them over while we were eating. I'm thinking I have the best friends in the world. We played the CD Ruben gave me first. LeeAnn rolled her eyes because mushy wasn't her favorite but she didn't argue with Robbie when he said, "Let's dance." Ruben and I started dancing where we left off at our Valentine's dance. I loved the slow dances best. Robbie likes the fast beat better so we danced a lot of both. The evening was so much fun I didn't want it to end. At 11:00 LeeAnn's Mom said it was time to go. Guess who got in the van first this time? Ruben wished me Happy Birthday again and kissed me several more times. I told him this was a great birthday and then I kissed him. Oh my gosh, CC. Ruben is so cool and I'm so amazed.

I thought I was tired but couldn't get to sleep. I kept thinking about Ruben and wondering what he's thinking and how high school is going to affect our going out with each other. Then I think I'm too young to worry about a boyfriend like this. Then I think, "But I really like him and what is wrong with having a boyfriend at 14?" I see TV shows where couples start liking each other in third grade and celebrate their 50th wedding anniversary. High school is making me a wreck.

Happy:    Ruben's kisses
Sad:       Tonight: High School

# JUNE 21

Dear CC,

I called Molly today and asked if she could meet me at the nursing home at ten o'clock tomorrow morning. She said she would be there. She asked if there was anything she could bring to help my plan. I told her just being there would be the best thing ever for my plan. She said she'd see me tomorrow.

I have no idea if Grandmother will respond or know who I am but I am not giving up. I have been seeing her regularly for a year and just want to try a few things to see if they make any difference. I also realize they may not. Molly was especially interested in the day that Grandmother Liz called the little girl "Carly". She thought that was significant.

I said, "I hope it transfers to me."

I got an email from Ruben today. We exchanged email addresses at LeeAnn's house the other night. He told me how much fun he had being part of my birthday party. He said he has been surprised at how much fun we have together no matter what we do. So he wanted to invite me to go someplace else with him. He said some of his friends that he practices football with want to take their dates to the Fourth of July celebration downtown next month. He suggested we ride the commuter train. He has ridden it several times and says the last train leaves in time for us to be back by eleven o'clock. He said he hoped I could go. He asked how my grandmother was doing. He said he hoped my plan worked.

He wrote, "Let me hear soon." and signed it "Your Friend, Ruben."

I started wondering how I would approach Mom. I'll remind her LeeAnn and I have ridden the train to a shopping mall. We just hadn't gone downtown by ourselves. But I wouldn't be by myself. I'd be with Ruben and a lot of football players. What would be safer than that? I think she will let me go but I never know. I'm 14 now and I think I'm responsible and use common sense. Mother says I'm so grown up with my relationship to Grandmother Liz. I hope she thinks I'm the same with Ruben. But Mother will probably think of something. Teenage girls have to pick the best times to ask their mothers for permission to do things. I'm not sure when the best time is with Mom. I'll have to think about this.

I decided to write Ruben back before I asked Mother. I thanked him for asking about the Fourth of July. I told him I haven't talked to my parents yet but was pretty sure they would let me go. It sounds like a lot of fun. I told him that I was going to the nursing home tomorrow and I was nervous about that. I told him that Grandmother's friend, Molly, was going with me. I thanked him again for the great CD and the fun evening of pizza, talking and dancing.

I said, "I had a perfect birthday and I'm glad you shared it with me." I told him I'd get back to him tomorrow about the Fourth. And signed it, "Your Friend, Carly."

Tomorrow will be stressful. I will be with Grandmother Liz and also have to ask Mother about going with Ruben.

LeeAnn is trying out for cheerleading but I have decided not to. I can yell but I can't jump. So my place is in the stands. She has been practicing every day and wears me out just watching her. She knows there is lots of competition in high school. I hope she wins because losing Ms. Personality was sad for her. I hope it made her stronger and more realistic about competition. We'll see.

Mother told me today we have our tickets to fly to Disney World. We leave the middle of July for a week. I'm excited about the trip. I just wish LeeAnn could go with us. I think I'll ask Mother about that too. But not tomorrow.

I've got all the things together I want to take with me to see Grandmother Liz. I put them all in the box I found. I have eight things. Her letter. The picture album Mother made for me. The two matching aprons. My baby doll. Grandmother's recipe book. Her brooch and a handkerchief. Of course my birthstone ring that I always have on makes nine. I'm ready for bed. I hope I sleep better tonight.

Happy:     Ruben
Sad:       Anxious

# JUNE 22

Dear CC,

I want to write about my day. It was very emotional in so many ways. It started out with a big surprise. Mother told me she had been talking to LeeAnn's mother and they have worked it out so LeeAnn can go with us to Disney World. Her mother said their family had wanted to go but haven't been able to and it would be great for LeeAnn to go with her best friend. They would pay her plane fare and contribute to the hotel room. LeeAnn would have money for her food, Disney World and spending money. I was so happy! I couldn't believe this was happening. I told Mother I had wanted to ask her and Dad if LeeAnn could go but had no idea they would think of it first.

Mother said, "You've always said you felt like an only child so we knew you would enjoy the trip more with someone your age."

And I'm thinking, "You and Dad will too." I can't wait to talk to LeeAnn.

Also this morning Mother asked me if I wanted her to be part of my plan. I had to admit I hadn't thought of that so I told her that was okay with me but it was up to her to decide. She said she would like to stay at the nursing home and be available if I wanted her if that would be okay. I said that would be great. I was wondering if her being in Grandmother's room would be a distraction rather than a help. But at this point I couldn't worry about that.

On the way to the nursing home I decided to ask Mother about the Fourth of July. I needed to break the tension I felt about my visit with Grandmother Liz. I told Mom that I wanted to change the subject from Grandmother for a minute. Before she could speak I dived right into my planned speech. I told Mother that Ruben has invited me to go downtown to the Fourth of July celebration.

"But you always watch it on television." I said I want to be on television this year and you can watch me. We looked at each other and smiled.

"You really like Ruben don't you?" I admitted I did. She said that she and Dad were concerned that 14 was awfully young to have a serious boyfriend. I asked what she meant by serious. She said spending a lot of time with him that takes away from your family and other friends. I said I had to disagree with that. I said I don't feel my time with Ruben interferes with my family and friends. I pointed out that every time I have gone out with Ruben I have been with other friends. She said she had forgotten that. I asked her to tell me something I have missed doing with her and Dad. She almost laughed and said she couldn't think of anything.

"Mom, I don't consider my dating Ruben that serious. Yes, I like him, but we're not getting married!" She said she and I probably have different meanings for the word serious. I definitely agreed with that.

I knew what was coming next. She said, "We don't want you riding in a car with a 16 year old driver."

"I know that and I won't be."

She looked surprised and asked, "So what is this plan?"

"The commuter train. We would be riding downtown with other friends of Ruben's and their dates and come back on the late train by eleven o'clock. Someone will pick us up and bring me home."

"So who is someone?"

"I don't know, but if you or Dad want to do that you could. Would you take Ruben home?"

"Of course."

I figured if I agreed to that part she was going to let me go.

"So what is your answer?" She said it was fine with her but I'd have to talk with Dad.

I asked her if she would do that part for me. "Then you can tell him our conversation and I won't have to go through it all again."

"So you want me to go through it all again?"

"Yes. You and Dad will have comments to make because you both think out loud and I won't have to listen to all the what if's." She agreed to talk to Dad and was sure it would be okay with him so the answer is yes. I smiled and said thank you. Sometimes parents can be very understanding and this was one of those times.

Knowing the answer to my next question, I looked over at Mom and said, "How old were you when you met Dad?"

She looked at me and said, "That isn't fair. We were both 12 but that was different."

I said, "No more questions." We both laughed out loud.

I couldn't wait to get home and email Ruben. Since I've already told him I'm sure I can go I don't think he'll be surprised. I'm so glad Mother and I could talk about Ruben without one of us getting upset. It was a very adult conversation and I really appreciated it. I feel now it may be easier to talk to Mom about my high school experiences. I'll have lots of questions and I will feel better asking her if we have this kind of comfort zone I'm feeling right now. I don't want Mother to be my best friend. I want her to be my best Mom. I've heard girls brag about their mothers being their best friend and then I meet them and they look just like their daughter. That would be embarrassing. I want my Mom to be the Mom that I love and enjoy being around. I know we'll disagree but LeeAnn and I disagree. That's not always a bad thing. I think Mother and I are starting high school on the right track.

I heard Mom say, "Aren't you going to get out of the car?"

"Oh my gosh! I didn't know we were here."

"You were really in deep thought".

I said, "Yes and you'd be surprised about who." We both smiled, thinking about different people.

Now I was ready to carry out the plan I had been working on for Grandmother Liz for almost a year. Sometimes I wonder why this idea has been so important to me. I hope today I will find the answer.

I chose morning because it is usually the best time for Grandmother. As I was walking down the hall I was getting cold feet and thinking there may be no good time. But my plan had kept me going this far and I wasn't about to give it up. We saw Molly and Marsha and they said they had been in to say hello to Grandmother. It was very obvious that Molly was shaken after seeing Grandmother.

Molly said to Mom, "I had no idea Liz was this bad. I'm so sorry." Mother asked her how long it had been since she had seen Liz.

Molly said, "About five years." We all agreed that in that amount of time Alzheimer's patients can change a lot. Each patient changes at a different pace but Grandmother's doctor said hers has progressed especially fast. I asked Molly if Grandmother knew her.

I saw the tears in Molly's eyes as she said, "No".

Marsha and Mom said they would be around. They both had books to read and Mother likes to visit with other patients sometimes. Mother said she would look in later and see if I wanted her to come in.

I walked in Grandmother's room and gave her a cheery hello and hug.

I said, "Carly is back." She immediately took my hand like she always does. I talked about Molly being there and said we wanted to talk to her today and show her some old things of hers. She looked at Molly and then at me. Molly and I sat down in folding chairs next to Grandmother. I opened my box and set the items on a TV tray next to Grandmother's "Everything Chair". I picked up the letter first. I told her that this was a very special letter that she wrote Carly on the day she was born. She whispered the word, "born." I said I wanted to read the letter to her. While I was reading it Molly had to leave the room because she couldn't control her crying. Grandmother sat with her head down and I wanted to be sure she wouldn't nod off so I would touch her hand every so often.

Molly came back in the room and sat back down next to Grandmother and took her hands in hers. When I finished the letter I handed it to Grandmother.

I said, "You wrote this letter to me, Carly, on the day I was born. My mother, Phyllis, gave it to me on my 13th birthday." Grandmother repeated the word "birthday." Next I asked Molly to help me. She put Grandmother's apron on Grandmother and I put mine on. I took the picture I wanted out of the album and put it on the TV tray. Grandmother looked at it. I pointed out that we now have on those aprons. She looked at the picture again and then at her apron and mine. She pointed to the picture and then looked at the aprons again. I told her the picture was when I, Carly, was a little girl and now I am 14. "The girl in the picture is this girl here." And I pointed to myself.

She looked at me and whispered "Carly." I reached over and gave her a hug. I wasn't sure if she understood or was just repeating. I wanted her to cross that line.

I opened her recipe book and put it in her lap. I told her she used to cook using this big book. "And I, Carly, helped you cook," and pointed to the picture again. She closed the book and handed it back to me. Before I could pick up the next item Grandmother reached over and picked up the baby doll. She has stuffed animals in her room so she has held small soft toys before. She looked at it and smiled. When she looks at something and smiles it always confuses me. I don't know if the smile means a memory flashed by or that she is enjoying the moment. I usually take it as enjoying the moment but maybe I need to pay more attention. Sometimes when I'm frustrated I want to say, "Grandmother you have on an ugly dress today" and see if she smiles. But I know I'll never be able to do that. I said, "Grandmother, Carly used to be the size of that doll but now she is all grown up and pointed to me."

She looked at the doll again and said, "Carly."

Molly looked at me and said, "Liz acts like she remembers Carly."

"She might, but does she know me now?" Molly just shook her head and said she didn't know.

Next I wanted Grandmother to see and hold her brooch and handkerchief. I know things like this must have had special meaning to her. She touched the brooch and handed it back to me. She looked at the handkerchief and put it in her pocket. I just said, "Do you like the handkerchief?" She gave me her usual smile. She has Kleenex in her room so she might have thought that was what it was. After seeing her keep the handkerchief, which was fine, I didn't want to take my ring off.

I took Grandmother's hand and said, "Grandmother Liz, Carly (pointing to myself) loves you very much. You are very special to me. I'm wearing our birthstone ring. We were both born in June. Did you want Carly to wear your birthstone ring?" She just held my hand, touched the ring and looked at it for a long time.

Just then Mother came to the doorway but didn't say anything. Grandmother Liz looked up at her, held my hand up and said, "Carly's ring". I looked at Grandmother wondering if what I heard was real and saw a tear fall on her cheek. That was all I needed. I started crying as did Molly and Mother. Marsha came in the room and wanted to know what had happened. Molly said she would tell her later. Grandmother looked scared like she didn't know what was happening. I hugged her and hugged her. She didn't hug back but that was okay. This time with Grandmother Liz was for me and I'm satisfied that she has some kind of memory of me, no matter how small, somewhere in her mind.

I learned in the Alzheimer's support group that with Alzheimer's we have no idea how much memory the patients have because they can't tell us when they are at this stage. And for the memories they do have, they probably wouldn't be able to find the words to share it. That part is the most frustrating to me. Some day someone has to figure out this Alzheimer's disease.

This disease is so cruel. But I do feel better now that Grandmother and I have both done the best we could to cope with it. The terrible struggle is hers and mine is to watch her go through it. I will continue to visit her as long as she lives. I have learned a lot about Grandmother Liz. She was a strong and wonderful lady, a good friend and mother. I'm glad my brothers are older and she was able to be a loving grandmother to them and to me even if for only a few years. I am so fortunate to have the letter she wrote. I continue to be amazed that she even thought to do that. I'm amazed at lots of things but the letter is really special. I think of other grandchildren that have a grandparent who has Alzheimer's and they don't have anything like my letter. My letter is important because it keeps a healthy Grandmother Liz alive for me to go to and enjoy anytime. I accept reality and know how Grandmother is today but I also have something else that I will cherish forever.

Two nurses came into the room wanting to know if everything was all right. We were laughing by now, embarrassed by all our crying, and told them we were all fine. We took the apron off Grandmother and I put all the things back in the box except the doll and handkerchief. Grandmother didn't want to part with them and that is fine. I can get the doll later. Molly gave me a big hug and said she is so proud of me and thinks I'm a brave young woman to do what I have done since I read Liz' letter. She said she had no idea why she and Liz decided to write those letters but was so glad they did. At least Molly got to share my letter with me. I told Molly I was just trying to be a granddaughter.

She smiled and said, "A really special granddaughter." I blushed and cried some more.

Mother and I told Molly and Marsha good-bye and thanked them for coming and being there with me today. Molly said she would keep in touch with Mother to find out how Liz is doing.

Mother and I got in the car and she asked, "Where do you want to have lunch?"

"I don't want food but I would like some ice cream."

Mother said, "Ice cream is food."

"No it's not. It's too good to be food." I suggested we go to the "50's Place" and have a double/trouble banana split. On the way Mother wanted to tease me and asked, "So who were you thinking about in the car earlier?"

"You really want to know?"

"Yes."

"You." I couldn't believe it but she blushed and then smiled.

When we got to the restaurant our conversation continued the same way as when we talked in the car this morning. But this time it was all about Grandmother Liz. I told Mother I hope I did the right thing today showing Grandmother her things and reading her the letter. I know it was more for me than for her but it was something I had to do.

Mother said when she gave me my Birth Day Letter a year ago she had no idea how it would affect me or if it would have any meaning at all to me, considering Grandmother's illness now.

Mom said, "But as the months went by I realized how important it became to you. I was worried that whatever you did with it you would be disappointed." I assured Mother I wasn't disappointed. I told her that to give me the letter was the right thing to do.

Mother told me she hated seeing me so frustrated over Grandmother's illness and had wished that she could help me but knew it was something I had to work out myself.

She said, "I believe you did that today!" I agreed. I feel that now I can visit Grandmother on her terms instead of mine. I have found out everything that I needed to know. I know Grandmother cannot communicate with me in a way I can understand. That is okay. Just to visit her will be enough now. I told Mother I loved her and Grandmother very much. I thanked Mother for being so patient with me through this journey I had to make. Mother reached over and touched my hand. I looked at my birthstone ring and began to cry. I don't know if it was because it's the ending of something or because it's the beginning.

Happy:     Beginnings
Sad:         Endings

# About The Author

Marci Holland was born in Wichita Falls, Texas, and grew up in Kansas City, Missouri. She is a graduate of Baker University, Baldwin, Kansas. She taught elementary and secondary school for twenty-four years. She is married, has three grown children: Shari, Michele and Mark, and four grandsons. She and her husband Ron are active in Trinity United Methodist Church, Kansas City, Kansas, where their son is the Senior Pastor. Marci and Ron are retired and living in Kansas City, Missouri.

Printed in the United States
26135LVS00004B/367-369